CAMBRIDGE LIBRARY COLLECTION

Books of enduring scholarly value

Polar Exploration

This series includes accounts, by eye-witnesses and contemporaries, of early expeditions to the Arctic and the Antarctic. Huge resources were invested in such endeavours, particularly the search for the North-West Passage, which, if successful, promised enormous strategic and commercial rewards. Cartographers and scientists travelled with many of the expeditions, and their work made important contributions to earth sciences, climatology, botany and zoology. They also brought back anthropological information about the indigenous peoples of the Arctic region and the southern fringes of the American continent. The series further includes dramatic and poignant accounts of the harsh realities of working in extreme conditions and utter isolation in bygone centuries.

Narrative of an Expedition to the Shores of the Arctic Sea in 1846 and 1847

In the mid-nineteenth century, the northern coastline of North America was of particular interest to the Hudson's Bay Company as it was believed to hold the key to the elusive North-West Passage, a trade route from the Atlantic to the Pacific. Recruited to lead a team to survey part of this forbidding region, the Scottish explorer John Rae (1813–93) undertook his first expedition during 1846–7. It was remarkable not only for its success, but also because Rae's was the first crew to overwinter in the Arctic. Unlike other Victorian explorers, Rae embraced the culture of the Inuit and learnt to live off the land like them, which enabled him to complete his survey. First published in 1850, this journal relates the details of his journey as well as how he and his men survived the extreme conditions. It remains a valuable document in the history of Arctic exploration.

Narrative of an Expedition to the Shores of the Arctic Sea in 1846 and 1847

John Rae

CAMBRIDGE
UNIVERSITY PRESS

CAMBRIDGE UNIVERSITY PRESS

Cambridge, New York, Melbourne, Madrid, Cape Town,
Singapore, São Paolo, Delhi, Mexico City

Published in the United States of America by Cambridge University Press, New York

www.cambridge.org
Information on this title: www.cambridge.org/9781108057813

© in this compilation Cambridge University Press 2013

This edition first published 1850
This digitally printed version 2013

ISBN 978-1-108-05781-3 Paperback

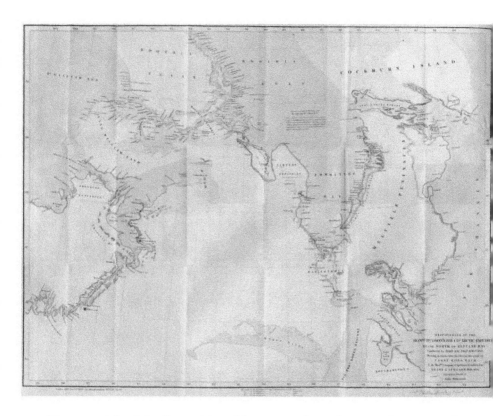

The material originally positioned here is too large for reproduction in this reissue. A PDF can be downloaded from the web address given on page iv of this book, by clicking on 'Resources Available'.

NARRATIVE

OF AN

EXPEDITION TO THE SHORES

OF

THE ARCTIC SEA

IN 1846 AND 1847.

By JOHN RAE,

HUDSON BAY COMPANY'S SERVICE, COMMANDER OF THE EXPEDITION.

WITH MAPS.

LONDON:

T. & W. BOONE, 29, NEW BOND STREET.

1850.

MARCHANT SINGER AND CO., PRINTERS, INGRAM-COURT,
FENCHURCH-STREET.

TO

SIR GEORGE SIMPSON,

Governor-in-Chief of Rupert's Land,

THE ZEALOUS PROMOTER OF ARCTIC DISCOVERY,

THIS VOLUME IS INSCRIBED

AS A TRIBUTE OF RESPECT AND REGARD

BY THE AUTHOR.

CONTENTS.

CHAPTER IV.

CHAPTER V.

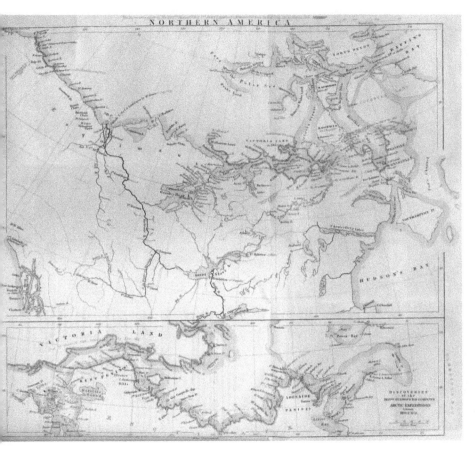

The material originally positioned here is too large for reproduction in this reissue. A PDF can be downloaded from the web address given on page iv of this book, by clicking on 'Resources Available'.

NARRATIVE,

ETC. ETC.

CHAPTER I.

Object and plan of the Expedition—Equipment at York Factory—
Boats—Crews— Articles useful in an Arctic Voyage—Break-
ing up of the ice in Hayes and Nelson Rivers—Departure from
York Factory—Progress retarded by the ice—First night at
sea—Reflections—Rupert's Creek—Unbroken fields of ice—
Broad River—Description of the coast—Double Cape Churchill
—Open sea to the north and north west—Arrive at Churchill—
White whales—Mode of catching them—Sir George Simpson's
instructions—Stock of provisions.

IT is already well known to those who take an
interest in Arctic discovery, that the Hudson's Bay
Company intended fitting out an expedition in 1840,
which was to have proceeded to the northern shores
of America by Back's Great Fish River, for the purpose of tracing the coast between the river Castor
and Pollux of Dease and Simpson, and the Strait of
the Fury and Hecla, as it was then very generally
supposed that Boothia was an island.

B

The party was to have been commanded by that able and enterprising traveller, Mr. Thomas Simpson, whose indefatigable exertions, in conjunction with those of Mr. Dease, had during the three preceding years effected so much; but his untimely and melancholy fate prevented that intention from being carried into effect, and the survey of the Arctic coast was discontinued for a few years.

When it was determined that the survey should be resumed, Sir George Simpson, Governor-in-Chief of the Company's territories, informed me that a boat expedition to the Arctic Sea was again contemplated, at the same time doing me the honour of proposing that I should take command of it,—a charge which I most joyfully accepted.

The plan of the expedition was different from any that had hitherto been adopted, and was entirely of Sir George Simpson's forming. Its leading features were as follows:—A party of thirteen persons, including two Esquimaux interpreters, was to leave Churchill in two boats at the disruption of the ice, and coast along the western shore of Hudson's Bay to the northward as far as Repulse Bay; or, if thought necessary, to the Strait of the Fury and Hecla. From this latter point the shore of the Arctic Sea was to be traced to Dease and Simpson's farthest discoveries eastward; or, if Boothia Felix should be found to form part of the American continent, up to some place surveyed by Captain or Commander (now Sir John and Sir James C.) Ross.

I started from the Sault de Ste. Marie in the latter part of July, 1845, in a canoe which I took on with me as far as Red River, where this frail vessel was changed for a boat, which is better adapted for traversing large sheets of water. We had rather a stormy passage to Norway House, at which place five men were engaged for the expedition; and having brought two with me from the southern department, I required only three more, who I knew could easily be procured at York Factory.

At first there was some difficulty in getting volunteers, as a report had got abroad (set on foot, I believe, by either M'Kay or Sinclair, guides and steersmen with the expeditions under Sir G. Back and Dease and Simpson), that the whole party, if not starved for want of food, would run the risk of being frozen to death for want of fuel.

After leaving Norway House our progress was slow, the water being very shallow, and our boat rather a heavy drag, for a single crew, over the portages. Two Indians who were engaged, the one to go as far as Oxford House, and the other all the way to York Factory, stipulated that they should do no work on Sunday; to which I readily agreed, thinking that they acted conscientiously; and this I really believe to have been the case with one; but I had some doubts about the sincerity of the other, when I learned that, before leaving us, he had stolen a shirt and blanket from one of the boat's crew.

We arrived at York Factory on the 8th October,

during a strong gale of north-east wind with heavy rain and sleet, which had thoroughly drenched us all; in addition to which the men were so bedaubed with mud whilst dragging the boats along shore, that scarcely a feature of their faces could be distinguished.

On landing I was most kindly welcomed by Chief-Factor Hargrave and the other gentlemen of the Factory.

There was little probability of our being able to get to Churchill by water this autumn, nevertheless the boats that had been built for the expedition were launched and put in order for sea. They were fine looking and strong clinker-built craft, 22 feet long by 7 feet 6 inches broad, each capable of carrying between fifty and sixty pieces of goods of 90 lbs. per piece. They were each rigged with two lug sails, to which a jib was afterwards added; under which, with a strong breeze of wind, they were found to work admirably. They were named the "North Pole" and the "Magnet."

We had a continuance of northerly winds until the ice began to form on the river, when it would have been highly imprudent to attempt going along the coast, and I did not wish to run the risk of having our boats stranded, which would have been a very likely occurrence had we put to sea. There was, therefore, nothing to be done but to haul our boats up again; nor did this cause me much disappointment, as I felt pretty certain that, in the following spring, we could advance as fast to the northward as the season of the breaking up of the ice did ; and this supposition I afterwards found to be correct.

My attention was now turned to the proper equipment of my party, in which I was most ably assisted by Chief-Factor Hargrave and my friend, Mr. W. Mactavish, who was in charge of York during the temporary absence of the former gentleman ; so that, with keeping a meteorological journal — in which the temperature of the air, height of the barometer, force and direction of the winds, and state of the weather were registered eight times a day — and taking observations for latitude, longitude, variation of the compass, and dip of the needle, &c., I had occupation enough on my hands.

Among other articles which I thought might be useful, were a small sheet-iron stove for each boat, a set of sheet-iron lamps for burning oil after the Esquimaux fashion, some small kettles (commonly called conjurors) having a small basin and perforated tin stand for burning alcohol, a seine net, and four small windows, each of two double panes of glass. An oiled canvass canoe was made, and we also had one of Halkett's air boats, large enough to carry three persons. This last useful and light little vessel ought to form part of the equipment of every expedition.

On the 30th April, 1846, that harbinger of spring, the Canada goose, was seen ; and so early as the 5th May the ice in Hayes' River commenced breaking up ; but it was more than a month after this date before the Nelson or North River opened. At length, on the 12th June, it was reported that a passage was practicable, and everything was got in readiness for making a start on the following day.

The crews of the boats were divided as follows:—

NORTH POLE.

John Rae.
John Corrigal, Orkneyman, Steersman.
Richard Turner, half-breed, Middleman.
Edward Hutchison, Orkneyman, ditto.
Hilard Mineau, Canadian,   ditto.
Nibitabo, Cree Indian,   ditto and hunter.

MAGNET.

George Flett, Orkneyman, Steersman.
John Folster,   ditto,   Middleman.
William Adamson, Zetlander,   ditto.
Jacques St. Germain, Canadian, ditto.
Peter Matheson, Highlander,   ditto.

All these men had the same wages, namely, £40 per annum, with the promise of a gratuity in the event of good conduct.

The lading of each of the boats, including the men's luggage, amounted to about seventy pieces; and with this cargo they were quite deep enough in the water and very much lumbered — so much so that, to allow room for pulling, a quantity of the cargo had to be displaced.

On the 13th June, after bidding farewell to our kind friends at York, and receiving a salute of seven guns and three hearty cheers, we set sail with a light air of fair wind. We had not proceeded more than a mile down the river, when the wind chopped round directly in our teeth, and blew a gale. As I could not think of turning back, we were speedily under close-reefed sails, turning to windward; the wind and tide were going in opposite directions, and there was an ugly cross sea running, which caused us to ship much water over both the lee and weather side. After a couple hours of this work we gained sufficient offing to clear the shallows, which lie for some miles out from the point of Marsh, (this being the name of the N.E. extremity of York Island), and stood across towards the north shore of the Nelson River. The men in the Magnet, having erroneously carried on too great a press of canvass, were left a mile or two astern. As we advanced the wind gradually abated, and we soon fell in with quantities of ice driving along with the current, through which we had much difficulty in finding a passage.

We made the land near Sam's Creek; and it being now calm, and flood tide strong against us, we cast anchor close to the shore between 9 and 10 o'clock. The night was beautiful, and, as all my men had gone to sleep, nothing interrupted the stillness around but the occasional blowing of a white whale, the rather musical note of the " caca wee " (long-tailed duck), or the harsh scream of the great northern diver. Yet I could not close my eyes. Nor was this wakefulness caused by the want of comfort in my bed, which I must own was none of the most inviting, as it consisted of a number of hard-packed bags of flour, over which a blanket was spread, so that I had to accommodate myself in the best way I could to the inequalities of the surface. To a man who had slept soundly in all sorts of places— on the top of a round log, in the middle of a swamp, as well as on the wet shingle beach, such a bed was no hardship; but thoughts now pressed upon me which during the bustle and occupation of preparation had no time to intrude. I could not conceal from myself that many of my brother officers, men of great experience in the Indian country, were of opinion that we ran much risk of starving; little was known of the resources of that part of the country to which we were bound; and all agreed that there was little chance of procuring fuel, unless some oil could be obtained from the natives. Yet the novelty of our route, and of our intended mode of operations, had a strong charm for me, and gave me an excitement which I could not otherwise have felt.

14th.—As there were great quantities of ice along the shore to the northward of us, I let the boats take the ground, so that this morning they were high and dry on the mud, the water being a mile or two outside of us, and we as far from the high-water mark.

As the Goose Hunt House (a small hut where one of the Company's servants and some Indians go every spring and autumn to shoot and salt geese,) was at no great distance, I visited it, but found that the people had taken their departure for the Factory —a certain sign that the geese and ducks had gone farther north. Numbers of the Hudsonian godwit (*limosa Hudsonica*) were flying about, apparently intending to breed in the neighbourhood.

The boats floated at a quarter after 10 A.M., and we got under weigh with a fine light breeze from the S.E. The temperature of the air was 62° and the water 40°. There were many pieces of ice floating about, and a great quantity close-packed about half a mile outside. At mid-day we were in latitude 57° 25′ 93″ N. After running by Massey's patent log for 10¾ miles north, we were stopped by ice at a few minutes after 1 P.M., when we made fast to a large grounded mass, which protected us from the smaller floating pieces as long as the tide was ebbing; but as soon as the flood made, it required all our exertions to prevent the boats being damaged. We now found the great advantage of some sheet copper that had been nailed on their bows, as it completely protected them from being chafed. At 11 next forenoon, finding our situation rather dangerous, as soon as the tide flowed far enough, we pushed inshore, and beached the boats on a fine smooth surface of mud and gravel. With the exception of a heavy shower of rain at 6 A.M., the weather continued fine all day, but the sky was too cloudy to permit any observations to be made.

On the 16th we advanced only 1½ miles. The temperature of the air 42° and the water 34°. By an azimuth of the sun the variation of the compass, 10° 54′ east, was obtained.

As it was only at, or near, high-water that we

could make any progress, we crept along shore about four miles during the morning's tide, and in the evening we put into Rupert's Creek, which afforded us good shelter, and also fresh water, of which we were getting rather short. A fresh breeze from the east brought in much ice, which completely blockaded our harbour. The morning of the 18th was very fine, but the easterly wind still continued, and such was the effect produced by it that not a spot of open water was to be seen. The latitude 57° 32′ 18″ was observed, and an observation of the sun's azimuth yesterday gave the variation of the compass 9° 56′ E. Some partridges *(tetrao saliceti)*, ducks, and a flat-billed phalarope *(P. fulicarius)* were shot.

19th.—The ice having become somewhat more open during the night, we left the creek at 4 A.M., and ran 32½ miles before a fine breeze of S.E. wind, through lanes of open water, as nearly as possible in a N.N.E. course. Large unbroken fields, on which numbers of seals were lying, now opposed our further progress. At high-water next morning, we set forward among ice so closely packed, that we were obliged to open a passage by pushing aside the smaller pieces; we thus gained between two and three miles and reached Broad River. We lay here during the remainder of the day, which was too cloudy for a meridian observation; but in the evening an amplitude of the sun gave variation 12° 19′ east. The dip of the needle was 84° 46′ 4″.

The morning's tide of the 21st advanced us nearly three miles. Our new position was found to be in latitude 58° 9′ 51″ N.; the latitude of Broad River must therefore be 58° 7′ N. A strong breeze of S.S.W. wind had driven out some of the ice, so that, with the aid of sails and poles, we gained 12 miles more northing in the evening.

From the 22nd to the 24th we continued to creep along-shore, but our progress was very slow, 19 miles being, at the highest estimate, as much as we gained. We were, however, killing ducks of various kinds, and collecting eggs enough to keep us in food. A deer was also shot by Nibitabo on the 22nd, and on the 24th I procured from a high mound of ice, where it was feeding, what appeared to be a Canada mithatch (*sitta Canadensis*). The skin was preserved, and is with other specimens in the Honourable Hudson's Bay Company's warehouse in London.

On the 25th we lay all day in a small creek, which afforded us a safe harbour.

The wind, which had yesterday blown a strong gale from the N.E., shifted round to W., which gave us some hopes of an opening to seaward. In the evening much ice drove out with the ebb. The latitude of our position by reduction to the meridian was 58° 31′ N.

26th.—This morning we were fortunate enough, after a great deal of trouble, to get the boats into comparatively open water, and as the wind was moderate from E.S.E. we threaded our way, through narrow channels and openings, until opposite Cape Churchill. At 3 P.M. we doubled the cape, and to our great joy found an open sea to the north and north west of it.

The whole of the coast between Nelson River and Cape Churchill is low and flat, with not a single rock in situ. There are, however, a number of boulder stones of granite, and debris of limestone, to be seen.

There are numerous lakelets near the shore, the banks of which form the favourite breeding places of the Canada goose, the mallard, pintail, teal, scaup, and long-tailed ducks, great northern diver,* and the Arctic tern. The phalaropus hyperboreus is also very numerous—so much so that I could have shot twenty in half-an-hour. The female of this phalarope and of the P. fulicarius is considerably larger, and has much finer markings on its plumage, than the male, the colours being much brighter.

As we sailed along shore to the westward, the land gradually became more high and rocky, and there were many ridges of stones lying off several miles from the beach, among which we had some trouble in threading our way, the navigation being rendered still more difficult by a thick fog.

---

* The male and female of the northern diver (*colymbus glacialis*) resemble one another so much that it is very difficult to distinguish the one from the other. The immature bird has often been described by ornithologists as the female.

We arrived at the mouth of Churchill River at 3 A. M. on the 27th, but as the tide was ebbing we could not stem the current, so that we did not reach the Company's Fort, situated on the west bank of the river and about five miles up, until half-past six, when I was most kindly welcomed by my friend Mr. Sinclair, chief trader, the gentleman in charge, who had not expected to see us so early.

My letter of instructions had not yet arrived, so that we took advantage of the delay thus occasioned to have the boats unloaded, some slight repairs effected, and the cargoes examined and dried. I determined on leaving here some tobacco, salt, and one or two other articles that were not absolutely essential, supplying their place with pemmican and flour. Some observations for the dip of the needle gave mean dip 84° 47′ 3″. The variation of the compass 12° 29′ east, and the latitude of the Establishment 58° 44′ 12″ were found, and the mean time of 70 vertical vibrations of the needle in the magnetic meridian was 148″.

The people of the fort were busy killing white whales, great numbers of which come up the river with the flood tide. The mode of taking them is very simple. A boat, having a harpooner both at bow and stern, sails out among the shoal, and being painted white, it does not alarm them; they approach quite close, and are thus easily struck. When harpooned they do not run any great distance in one direction, but dart about much in the way that a trout does when hooked.

On the evening of the 4th July the anxiously expected instructions arrived from Red River, viâ York Factory. The following is a copy of them :—

" Red River Settlement,

" Sir,   " 15th June, 1846.

"You are aware that the grand object of the expedition which has been placed under your direction is to complete the geography of the northern shore of America, by surveying the only section of the same that has not yet been traced, namely, the deep bay, as it is supposed to be, stretching from the western extremity of the Straits of the Fury and Hecla to the eastern limit of the discoveries of Messrs. Dease and Simpson.

" 2. For this purpose you will proceed from Churchill with the two boats, and twelve men that have been selected for this arduous and important service, losing not a moment, at least on your outward voyage, in examining such part of the coast as has already been visited and explored. In a word, you will reach, with as little loss of time as possible, the interesting scene of your exclusive labours.

" 3. In prosecuting the survey in question, you will, as a matter of course, endeavour to ascertain as accurately as circumstances may permit, without occasioning any serious delay, the latitudes and longitudes of all the most remarkable points within

the range of your operations, and also the general
bearing and extent of all the intermediate portions
of coast, embodying the whole at the same time in
the form of a chart, or rather of the draft of a chart,
from day to day.

" 4. But in addition to this, your principal and
essential task, you will devote as much of your
attention as possible to various subordinate and
incidental duties. You will do your utmost, con-
sistently with the success of your main object, to
attend to botany and geology; to zoology in all its
departments; to the temperature both of the air and
of the water; to the conditions of the atmosphere
and the state of the ice; to winds and currents; to
the soundings as well with respect to bottom as
with respect to depth; to the magnetic dip and the
variation of the compass; to the aurora borealis and
the refraction of light. You will also, to the best
of your opportunities, observe the ethnographical
peculiarities of the Esquimaux of the country; and
in the event of your wintering within the Arctic
Circle, you will be careful to notice any characteristic
features or influences of the long night of the high
latitudes in question. These particulars, and such
others as may suggest themselves to you on the
spot, you will record fully and precisely in a journal,
to be kept, as far as practicable, from day to day,
collecting at the same time any new, curious, or
interesting specimens, in illustration of any of the
foregoing heads.

" 5. In order to provide against the probable necessity of requiring two seasons for your operations, you will take with you all the provisions that your boats can carry, with such shooting, hunting, and fishing tackle as may enable you to husband your supplies. I need hardly mention medicines and warm clothing among the necessaries of your voyage, for, in full reliance on your professional zeal and ability, I place the health of your people, under Providence, entirely in your hands.

" 6. In the event of wintering in the country, you will cultivate the most friendly relations with the natives, taking care, however, to guard against surprise. For this purpose you will repeatedly and constantly inculcate on your men, collectively and individually, the absolute necessity of mildness and firmness, of frankness and circumspection.

" 7. If, in the event of your being unable to accomplish the whole of your task in one season, you see ground for doubting whether the resources of the country are competent to maintain the whole of your people, you will in that case send back a part of them to Churchill with one of the boats. For the remaining part of your men you cannot fail to find subsistence, animated as you and they are by a determination to fulfil your mission at the cost of danger, fatigue, and privation. Wherever the natives can live, I can have no fears with respect to you, more particularly as you will have the advantage of the Esquimaux, not merely in your actual supplies, but also in the means of recruiting and renewing them.

" 8. During the winter you will pursue the various objects of the expedition by making excursons, with a due regard, of course, to safety, on the snow or on the ice ; and at the close of your second season, after having accomplished the whole of your task, you will return according to your own discretion, either by your original course or by Back's Great Fish River, keeping constantly in view, till you reach Churchill or Great Slave Lake, the general spirit of these your instructions.

" 9. In conclusion, let me assure you that we look confidently to you for the solution of what may be deemed the final problem in the geography of the northern hemisphere. The eyes of all who take an interest in the subject are fixed on the Hudson's Bay Company ; from us the world expects the final settlement of the question that has occupied the attention of our country for two hundred years ; and your safe and triumphant return, which may God in His mercy grant, will, I trust, speedily compensate the Hudson's Bay Company for its repeated sacrifices and its protracted anxieties.

" I remain,

" Sir, &c.

(Signed)   " G. SIMPSON."

" John Rae, Esq.

   " Churchill,

     " Hudson's Bay."

c

The boats were loaded during the night, and at 6 A.M. were sent down to the old stone fort at the mouth of the river, where they were to wait for me a few hours. Besides an abundant supply of ammunition, guns, nets, twines, &c. for our own use, and various articles for presents and to barter with the Esquimaux, we had on board

20 bags pemmican, about 90 lbs. each,
2 ditto grease, ,, 90 lbs. ,,
25 ditto flour, each 1 cwt.
4 gallons of alcohol for fuel ;

with a good stock of tea, sugar, and chocolate, but only four gallons of brandy and two gallons of port wine, as I was well aware of the bad effects of spirits in a cold climate. Considering that we were to be absent fifteen or perhaps twenty-seven months, our quantity of provisions (amounting in all to little more than four months' consumption at full allowance) was not very great.

CHAPTER II.

HAVING taken on board Ouligbuck and one of his
sons as Esquimaux interpreters, and bid adieu to
Mr. Sinclair, who, during our stay, had omitted
nothing that could in any way tend to the comfort of
the party, we set sail at 11 o'clock on the 5th July
with a light air of N.N.E. wind, and stood to the
westward across Button's Bay. The weather was
fine, and to enliven the scene numbers of white
whales were seen sporting about, and sometimes
coming within a few yards of the boats. The men
were all in excellent health and spirits, there not

being a melancholy look nor a desponding word to be seen or heard among them.

At 3.30 P.M. we passed Pauk-a-thau-kis-cow River, and the wind having freshened and shifted round to the S.E. we had run upwards of forty miles before 10 o'clock. The temperature of the air was 49°, and of the water 50°, thus showing that there was little or no ice in the neighbourhood.

The night being fine we continued under sail, the crews being divided into two watches. The land had now become much lower than it was about Churchill, and the coast very flat; so that it was necessary to keep six or eight miles from the land when the tide was out; and even then, although the boats drew only two and a half feet water, there was little enough for them. The bottom was of mud, sand, or shingle, with every here and there a large boulder stone, some of them ten or twelve feet high.

Early on the morning of the 6th three Esquimaux came off in their kayaks, and although we were going at the rate of four miles an hour they easily overtook us. As they were going towards Churchill, I sent a few lines to Mr. Sinclair by them.

Our latitude at noon was 60° 17′ 59″ N. Thermometer in air 49°, in water 45°. The total distance run, measured by Massey's log, was ninety-five miles, which agreed very nearly with our latitude, the difference being easily accounted for by the circumstance that the ebb tide runs much stronger to the northward than the flood does in an opposite direction.

In the afternoon there was a strong breeze, which, although fair, was rather too much onshore and raised a heavy sea. At 5 P.M., having run twenty-five miles since noon, we got into shallow water, and although the heads of the boats were immediately turned to seaward, the ebb tide was too quick for us, and we got aground, being ten miles from the main shore. Five miles N.W. of us there was a small but steep island, on the E. side of which there was still a deep snow drift. By a meridian altitude of the moon our latitude was 60° 47′ 24″ N.

The following morning we floated at 2 A.M., and with a strong breeze from S.E. stood on our course. The weather looked threatening, and we had not been long out before the wind increased to a gale, and the sea rose in proportion. The boats fully realised the good opinion we had of them, but being so deeply laden the sea broke frequently over them, and kept us continually baling; at last the Magnet shipped a heavy sea, and the steersman, either from losing his presence of mind or from not knowing how to act, allowed the boat to broach to. Fortunately no other sea struck her whilst thus placed, else both she and the crew must inevitably have been lost. I here saw the benefit of the precaution I had taken to have some Orkneymen with me, for it was evident the others (although as good fellows as could possibly be wished) knew nothing about the management of a boat in such weather.

I was loath to lose so fine an opportunity of getting on, but it would have been recklessness to attempt proceeding. We accordingly ran in towards Knap's Bay, which was nearly abreast of us, and were soon anchored in a snug cove under the lee of the largest island in the bay. It was well that we put in here, for the wind in a short time increased to a perfect storm with heavy rain.

On a neighbouring island some miles to the south of us, many Esquimaux tents were seen, but we could not discover if they were inhabited.

Notwithstanding the rain I took my gun and made a tour of the island. It is about two miles long, a quarter of a mile broad, and not exceeding 100 feet in height, being covered with a scanty vegetation, and thickly strewn in many places with fragments of granite.

I met with a great many Esquimaux graves, the bodies being protected from wild animals by an arch of stone built over them. We found a number of spear-heads, knives, &c. placed in some of these heaps of stones; but the Esquimaux do not, I believe, destroy all the property of the deceased, as is common among most tribes of Indians.

Tracks were seen of a large white bear which had evidently been feasting on the eggs of various wild-fowl that breed here; among these I noticed the eider duck (*fuligula mollissima*), the long-tailed duck (*fuligula glacialis*), and the black guillimot (*uria grylle*).

In the evening, when the wind had somewhat

moderated, we were visited by five Esquimaux from the tents before mentioned; they each received a piece of tobacco, of which they are remarkably fond; and one of them promised to carry or forward to Churchill a letter which I addressed to Sir George Simpson. In a net that we had set, a salmon weighing 10 lbs. was caught. A large and deep river empties its waters into this bay; its course is about due east, and it abounds with salmon, seals, and white whales, being consequently a favourite resort of the natives. The rise of the tide was thirteen feet. When about to go to bed I found my blankets quite wet by the seas that washed over me in the morning; this, however, made them keep out the wind better, and did not certainly affect my rest.

The following day was more moderate, but it was 2 P.M. before we could venture out of our harbour. By observation the latitude 61° 9′ 42″ N., and the variation of the compass 7° 48′ east were obtained; the dip of the needle being 86° 18′ 3″ N.

At 4 A.M. on the 9th the wind went round so far to the east that we could not lie our course; it rained heavily, but the wind became more favourable, and we stood over towards the north shore of Nevill's Bay. The temperature of the water at mid-day 37°, air 44°; latitude by observation 61° 55′ 40″ N.

We passed among many small islands, the resort of great numbers of the birds already mentioned, which we used as food (although not very palatable) to save our pemmican. I also noticed a few of the foolish guillimot (*uria troile*), the first we had met with.* At half-past five, it being calm, we landed on a small island to get some water; we found a few Hutchins geese here, one of them having a brood of young with her. These appear to have taken the place of the Canada goose, as I have not seen any of the latter lately. At 8 o'clock, it still being calm, we pulled up towards the north point of Nevill's Bay, which bore east of us. No ice was to be seen, but there were numerous patches of snow on the main shore N.E. of us, distant 10 or 11 miles.

I saw a young shore lark and a young snow bunting, both able to fly. There are quantities of red, grey, and blue granite in this island, variegated with quartz.

The shores had now become steep and rugged, the whole coast being lined with bare primitive rocks.

---

* These birds breed in great numbers among the rocks in Orkney, and are much attached to their young. By chasing the latter in a boat they become so fatigued as to be easily caught. When one of them is taken into the boat the parent bird approaches within a few feet, dives under and around the boat in all directions, and whenever it comes up to the surface utters a peculiarly melancholy note, at the same time turning its head in a listening attitude as if expecting to hear an answer from the prisoner. The anxiety of the mother has always the desired effect, and it is pleasing to observe the joy with which she swims away with her recovered young one, nestling it under her wing and never permitting it to stray a foot from her.

After breakfast next morning we pulled round the east end of some rocks near which we had lain at anchor during the flood tide, and kept on our course across Whale Cove. Some small pieces of ice were seen floating about; the thermometer in the shade 55°, water 36°. A fog, which had been thick all the morning, cleared up at half-past ten, and we saw some islands at no great distance right a-head, and a smoke a few miles inland on our beam, probably made by Esquimaux, but we could not see any tents. Our latitude by observation was 62° 11′ 23″ N. Temperature of air 55°, of water 37°.

The weather was very variable, with calms and light breezes alternately. At a little after 7 in the evening we were off the south point of Corbet's Inlet. It rained hard almost all night; we, however, continued our course, and at 7 A.M. got among a number of reefs and islands that lie near the south point of Rankin's Inlet. In attempting to pass between two of these our boat got aground, and as the tide was ebbing she could not be shoved afloat again; but, as the greater part of the cargo was carried on shore before the water fell very far, no damage was done. An excellent observation of the sun gave latitude 62° 35′ 47″ N., variation 6° 6′ W., Marble Island bearing east by compass. The black guillimot was in such numbers here that four or five were killed at one shot. Many eggs were collected, and one nest was found having two eider and three long-tailed ducks' eggs in it. The eider had possession, but whether the birds had a mutual understanding, or whether the stronger had driven out the weaker possessor, it is difficult to say.

At 4 P.M. we floated and ran across the inlet, the traverse being 15 miles. We landed at its north point, as the wind and tide were both against us. There were numerous signs that this place is often visited by the Esquimaux; the bones of various animals and the remains of some stone " caches " being every where visible. A little before midnight a deer was shot by Corrigal. During a walk I fell in with a large white owl (*strix nyctra*). As is usually the case it was very shy, and could not be approached within gun-shot.*

The rise of the tide was 14 feet.

At half-past two A.M. on the 13th we landed at

---

* An excellent plan of shooting these birds, and one that I have often successfully practised, is to roll up a bit of fur or cloth about the shape and size of a mouse, and drag it after you with a line twenty yards long. The owl will soon perceive the decoy, although half-a-mile distant; and after moving his head backwards and forwards as if to make sure of his object, he takes wing, and making a short sweep in the rear of his intended prey, pounces upon and seizes it in his claws, affording the sportsman a fine opportunity of knocking him down. I have sometimes missed my aim, leaving the owl to fly away with the false mouse (which the sudden jerk had torn from the line) in his claws. The Indians, taking advantage of this bird's propensity to alight on elevated spots, set up pieces of wood in the plains or marshes with a trap fastened to the top. In this way I have known as many as fifty killed in the early part of winter by one Indian. The owl is very

Jalabert. The morning was delightful, being quite calm with a sharp frost. While we lay here waiting the change of the tide, Ouligbuck shot a fine large buck. Many seals were sporting about, and a shoal of salmon were seen swimming close to the beach. Having taken on board our venison, we pulled with the tide now in our favour. We saw upwards of a dozen Greenland whales, all apparently busy feeding, some of them very large. At noon we were in latitude 63° 6' 14″ N. The variation of the compass 8° 52' W. In the evening we passed Chesterfield Inlet. Great numbers of rocks lie out fully eight miles from the shore on its north side. The wind continued fair and moderate all night, and at 6 in the morning, when in the large bay S.W. of Cape Fullerton, a single Esquimaux visited us in his kayak. He had been at Churchill last year, but did not intend to go thither this season, although he had a number of wolf, fox, and parchment deer skins at his tent. A present of a knife and a piece of tobacco made him quite happy, and he left us shouting so loudly as to show that his lungs were in good order. The party to which he belongs consists of ten families, their hunting-grounds being situated on the borders of Chesterfield Inlet, where they spear a great number of deer whilst swimming across

daring when hungry. I remember seeing one of these powerful birds fix its claws in a lapdog when a few yards distant from the owner, and only let go his gripe after a gun was fired. The poor little dog died of its wounds in a few days.

28

in the autumn. At some distance inland, woods are found. A number of walruses were observed lying on a small ridge of rocks. They were grunting and bellowing—making a noise which I fancy would much resemble a concert of old boars and buffaloes. We did not disturb their music. Obtained a meridian observation of the sun, which gave latitude 64° 3′ 42″ N. As the refraction was great and the natural horizon used, this is probably erroneous; if it is not, Cape Fullerton is not properly laid down in the charts, being too far to the south. Temperature of the air 58°, water 41°.

When doubling Cape Fullerton, we were obliged, by the numerous granite reefs, to keep six or seven miles from the mainland. At 7 in the evening we landed to replenish our water casks, and had an unsuccessful chase after two deer. The horizon being clear, I saw Cape Kendall on Southampton Island, bearing S.E. by S. magnetic.

15th. We made but little progress last night, there being no wind. The weather was rather cold, the thermometer standing at 40°, and the water being only 4° above the freezing point indicated the proximity of ice. A short time afterwards a large *pack* was seen about five miles distant. On approaching nearer, we found that it extended along shore as far as the eye could see. At 2 p.m. we ran inshore, and took shelter under some grey-coloured granite rocks twenty feet high. Deer being noticed at no great distance, two or three sportsmen went after them, and succeeded in shooting a doe. A very large whale was observed.

Finding our present position far from being a safe one, at high water we pushed along shore among masses of ice during a thick fog, and entered an inlet which opportunely presented itself, and which proved to be an excellent harbour about 200 yards wide, from four to six fathoms deep, and nearly four miles long. The bottom being sand and mud would afford excellent anchorage for much larger craft than ours. As there were many seals swimming about, I was led to infer that salmon or trout were abundant; two nets were put down, but no fish were caught.

During a two days' detention here I traced, for eight miles, the course of a considerable river which empties its waters into the inlet. I found it to be a succession of rapids and deep pools, and running as nearly as possible in a S.S.E. course. Near its mouth upwards of thirty seals were lying basking in the sun; a ball fired among them sent the whole party walloping into the water at a great rate, more frightened, however, than hurt. One of the men had accompanied me, and during our walk we met with a hen partridge (*tetrao rupestris*) and her brood. I have seen many birds attempt to defend their young, but never witnessed one so devotedly brave as this mother; she ran about us, over and between our feet, striking at our hands when we attempted to take hold of her young, so that she herself was easily made prisoner. Although kept in the hand some time, when let loose again she continued her attacks with unabated courage and perseverance, and was soon left mistress of the field, with her family safe around her.

We were fortunate in finding some willows fully an inch in diameter, which were far superior for fuel to the sea-weed and short heath we had been using for the last two days.

Hutchins geese breed here in numbers, and as no Canada geese were seen, I presume that they do not usually come so far north along the coast. The shores have a very rugged appearance, there being numerous high ridges of primitive rocks running far out into the sea in an east and west direcrection, the line of stratification dipping to the south at an angle of 75° with the horizon. In many places these rocks were thickly studded with small garnets. The rise and fall of the tide was 13½ feet.

During the whole of the 16th the weather was cloudy, and it rained heavily all night; but on the 17th the wind increased to a gale, the sky cleared up, and a satisfactory observation was obtained by the artificial horizon, which placed us in latitude 64° 6′ 45″ N. As we were more than ten miles north of the situation where I had observed the latitude on the 14th, the difference between the latitude obtained then and that of our present situation shews the uncertainty of observations made with the natural horizon when there is much refraction, or when there is ice in the neighbourhood. The variation of the compass was 20° 10′ W. The gale continued all day, and being from the westward much ice was driven off shore.

18th. Last night the wind moderated a little, but about 2 A.M. it blew more strongly than before. The forenoon was sufficiently fine to permit me to observe the dip of the needle 86° 36′ 5″ N.

In the afternoon, when collecting plants, I discovered some willows of a larger growth than those we had before found, and I carried a load of them to the boat. In the evening there was no ice to be seen either along shore or in the offing, but it still blew too hard for us to get under weigh. The temperature of the air to-day varied from 50° to 55°. Just as I had turned in for the night, it was reported that two white bears were close at hand. I immediately got up, and set off " sans culottes" to have a share of the anticipated sport, when I soon discovered that two harmless deer in their winter coats had been mistaken for bears. It was high water to-day at 11h. 40m. A.M., the rise being 15 feet. By this it will appear that 3 o'clock is the time of high water at full and change of the moon.

At 3 next morning, the wind having moderated, we started, and ran along shore at a fine rate for ten miles; but here the coast turning more to the westward we could not lie our course, and were compelled to put ashore until the flood tide made ; for it was found that, contrary to what we had previously experienced, the current ran to the northward during the flow of the tide, and in an opposite direction during the ebb, this being probably caused by the strait north of Southampton Island being blocked up with ice. After an hour's stay we got under weigh again at a few minutes after seven, and turned to windward. Our latitude at noon was 64° 20′ 51″ N. It now fell calm; but this had not continued more than half an hour before a light breeze sprung up from the east, and at 1 P.M. we passed Whale Point. A great many whales were seen to-day, and one of them was swimming amongst a large flock of king ducks, apparently amusing itself with the confusion that it caused when rising to breathe. Temperature of the air 50°— water 38°.

20th. It being calm for some time during the night, we came to anchor whilst the tide was against us; but at 6 A.M. we again continued our route. There was much ice lying along the shore of Southampton Island, its proximity being indicated by the temperature of the water (35°) this morning. Some more large whales were noticed. The ice was again too close packed to permit us to advance; we therefore landed, and the latitude 64° 56′ 33″ N., and the variation of the compass 36° 13′ W., were observed. The musquitoes were very numerous and troublesome, but, nevertheless, the sportsmen succeeded in shooting five deer.

On the 21st and 22d we had a continued struggle

amongst heavy and close-packed ice until we reached Wager River Estuary, where we were detained all day by the immense quantities driving in with the flood and out again with the ebb tide, which ran at the rate of 7 or 8 miles an hour, forcing up the floes into large mounds, and grinding them against the rocks, with a noise resembling thunder.

During the ebb tide the eddy currents once or twice brought in the ice with great force, which would have smashed our boats, as they lay in rather an exposed situation along the face of some steep rocks, had it not fortunately taken the ground before it reached us. During our stay, a meridian observation of the sun by artificial horizon gave latitude 65° 15′ 36″ N., variation 48° 13′ W.

23d. There was a thin coat of ice on the water this morning, the temperature of which at midnight was 2° below the freezing point, that of the air 36°. As our position was far from safe, we were kept on the alert all night, and got under weigh at half-past three, for the purpose of finding some safer harbour. To get to a small bay a mile and a half to the west of us, we had more than once to pull for our lives, as the eddy currents already spoken of caused such sudden and uncertain movements among the ice that there was no telling on what side we were to expect it. With much difficulty we entered our harbour, and pulled half a mile up, so as to be safe from the ice, which we had reason to expect

34

would come in with the flood. The latitude of our new anchorage was 65° 16′ 8″ N. This is the most northerly point on the south side of Wager River, which appears to be not very correctly laid down in the charts. The channel is not more than four or five miles broad. In the evening, being wearied with delay, as soon as the flood tide slacked, we pushed out into the stream, and when in mid-channel had the advantage of a fine breeze, which enabled us to stem the current that still ran at the rate of five miles an hour. The boats had some narrow escapes, and the Magnet received a severe squeeze, but fortunately sustained no injury, and we were soon in safety on the north side of the channel.

24th. Having pulled along shore all night, we cast anchor at half-past five this morning to take breakfast and give rest to the men. Our course since crossing Wager River had been among a number of small rocky islands, between which we had some difficulty in threading our way, but we did not see any signs of a second opening into Wager Bay, although a sharp look-out was kept. A light air of fair wind springing up, we got under weigh at a few minutes before 8, and stood on to the northward, the ebb tide again running with us. At mid-day the temperature of the air was 45°, water 32°.

In the afternoon the breeze increased, and at a quarter-past seven we rounded Cape Hope, and ran into Repulse Bay. By an amplitude of the sun whilst setting, the variation of the compass 62° 40′

W. was obtained. As soon as we passed the Cape a great change in the temperature of the air and water was observed, the former being 56°, and the latter 46°.

25th. We continued under sail all night, and at 6 in the morning were within seven miles of the head of the Bay, and cast anchor between a small island and the shore to get some fuel and cook breakfast. Our latitude was 66° 26′ 57″ N. Variation of compass 59° 10′ W.

In the afternoon, the wind being ahead, we plied to windward, and when entering Gibson's Cove, observed with much joy four Esquimaux on the shore. I immediately landed near them, and taking Ouligbuck's son with me as interpreter, joined the party, and calling out Texma (peace), shook hands with them. They were at first in great fear, and appeared half inclined to run away, but on our kind intentions towards them being explained they became quite at ease, chatting and laughing as if we had been old acquaintances. They were good-looking, of low stature, and much more cleanly than those in Hudson's Straits. Their dresses were made of deer skin, of the form so often described, the coat having a long tail somewhat resembling that of an English dress coat. Their legs were encased in waterproof boots made of seal-skin, and they all wore mittens, which they seldom took off their hands. There were two of them middle-aged, Oo-too-ou-ni-ak (who had a formidable beard and whiskers) and Kir-ik-too-oo ; the other two were lads from eighteen to twenty years of age ; and we were soon after joined by a fine young fellow with ruddy cheeks and sparkling black eyes, having an expression of exceeding good humour in his laughing countenance. Our new friend wore round his head a narrow leather band of deer-skin ornamented with foxes' teeth, and appeared to be somewhat of a dandy in his own estimation. None of the party had ever visited Churchill, and they had neither heard nor seen anything of Sir John Franklin. From a chart drawn by one of the party, I was led to infer that the sea (Akkoolee), to the west of Melville Peninsula, was not much more than forty miles distant in a N.N.W. direction, and that about thirty-five miles of this distance was occupied by deep lakes ; so that we would have only five miles of land to haul a boat over—a mode of proceeding which, even had the distance been much greater, I had intended adopting, in preference to going round by the Fury and Hecla Straits.

A small river empties its waters into the Bay within a hundred yards of the place where we landed : this stream, up which the boat was to be dragged, issues from one of the lakes through which we had to pass. Leaving all the men but one to unload the boats, I went some miles inland to trace our intended route. After walking about five miles along the stream already mentioned (the current in which was very strong), we arrived at the first lake, a long and narrow body of water, having steep and in some places rocky banks, which we traced for two miles, and returned late in the evening to our companions.

CHAPTER III.

Receive a visit from a female party—Their persons and dress described—Crossing the Isthmus—Drag one of the boats up a stream—Succession of rapids—North Pole Lake—Find a plant fit for fuel—Christie Lake—Flett Portage—Corrigal Lake—Fish—Deer-scaring stones—White wolf—Stony Portage—View of the sea—Exploring parties sent in advance—Their report—Long Portage—Difficult tracking—Miles Lake—Muddy Lake—Rich pasturage and great variety of flowers on its banks—Marmot burrows—Salt Lake—Visit Esquimaux tents—Discouraging report of the state of the ice—Esquimaux chart—Reach the sea—Ross inlet—Point Hargrave—Cape Lady Pelly—Stopped by the ice—Put ashore—Find a sledge made of ship-timber—Thick fog—Wolves—Walk along the shore—Remains of musk-cattle and reindeer—Nature of the coast—Danger from the ice—Irregular rise of the tide—Deer on the ice—Fruitless efforts to proceed northward—Cross over to Melville Peninsula—Gale—Again stopped by the ice—Dangerous position of the boat—Return to starting point—Meeting with our Esquimaux friends at Salt Lake—Deer begun to migrate southward—Walk across the isthmus to Repulse Bay.

THE morning of the 26th was fine, with a fresh breeze from W.N.W. A visit which I had intended paying to the ladies was anticipated by their coming over to our side of the river, bag and baggage.

They were accompanied by a very old man named
Shad-kow-doo-yak, who was extremely infirm, being
obliged to move about in an almost horizontal pos-
ture, supported by a stick. There were six women,
(three old, the other three young,) the whole of them
married. One of the latter appeared quite like a
girl of ten years, and was rather good-looking, having
more regular features, and being cleaner and more
neat in her dress than the others. They were all
tatooed on the face, the form on each being nearly
the same, viz. a number of curved lines drawn from
between the eyebrows up over the forehead, two
lines across the cheek from near the nose towards
the ear, and a number of diverging curved lines
from the lower lip towards the chin and lower jaw.
Their hands and arms were much tatooed from the
tip of the finger to the shoulder. Their hair was collected in two large bunches, one on each side of the
head; and a piece of stick about ten inches long and
half-an-inch thick being placed among it, a strip of
different coloured deer-skin is wound round it in a
spiral form, producing far from an unpleasing effect.
They all had ivory combs of their own manufacture,
and deer-skin clothes with the hair inwards; the
only difference between their dresses and those of
the men being that the coats of the former had much
larger hoods, (which are used for carrying children,)
in having a flap before as well as behind, and also
in the greater capacity of their boots, which come

40

high above the knee, and are kept up by being fastened to the girdle. Some needles, beads, and other trifles were given them, at which they manifested their joy with loud shouts and yells, differing from the men in this respect, who received what was given them in silence, although they were evidently much pleased.

In the forenoon we were joined by two fine-looking young fellows who had just returned from hunting deer, in which they had been successful, having driven a large buck off one of the islands into the water and speared it there.

One of the women had been on board the Fury and Hecla, both at Igloolik and Winter Island, and still wore round her wrist some beads which she had obtained from these vessels. This party consisted of twenty-six individuals, there being four families.

All the cargo being placed in security and the Magnet well moored in our little land-locked harbour, the party, assisted by four Esquimaux, commenced dragging the North Pole up the stream.

The latitude of our landing place was found to be 66° 32′ 1″ N., being about seven miles further south than it has been laid down on the charts. The variation of the compass by an azimuth was 58° 37′ 30″ W. This I afterwards found to be erroneous, probably arising from local attraction. The rate of the chronometer had become so irregular that it could not be depended upon for finding the longitude, and during the winter it stopped altogether.

When about to put on a pair of Esquimaux boots, one of our female visitors, noticing that the leather of the foot was rather hard, took them out of my hands and began chewing them with her strong teeth. This is the mode in which they prepare and soften the seal skin for their boots, and they are seldom without a piece of leather to gnaw when they have no better occupation for their teeth. At half-past nine P.M. the men returned from the boat, having been absent since half-past seven in the morning. They had with much labour dragged her three miles through a succession of rapids, the channel being so obstructed with large boulder stones and rocks, that the most of the party were obliged to be almost continually up to the waist in ice-cold water. The boat had received some severe blows and rubs, but no material damage. The worst part of the river had been passed, and it was only a mile and a-half farther to the lake (named by the Esquimaux Chi-gi-uwik) from which it takes its rise. The Esquimaux who had assisted us were paid with a large knife each.

Two nets that had been set produced four salmon, but the best season for catching these fish was over, as they had now returned to deep water. The evening was cloudy with a strong and chilly breeze from N.N.W. Temperature of the air at 10 P.M. 35°.

27th. As soon as the men had finished breakfast they carried each a load over the rocks to where the boat lay.

I this morning tried some of our male friends with a little tea and biscuit, which they did not relish nearly so well as the ladies had done the previous evening. Indeed, one of the latter, whom I have already mentioned, knew what biscuit was the moment she saw it, and said she had eaten some when on board Captain Parry's ships. I remained at our landing-place until the afternoon to obtain some observations. That for latitude gave a result different only 4″ from that of yesterday. Having engaged three Esquimaux to carry up some things that were still to be taken, at one o'clock I followed my men and came up with them some distance up the lake. As we could not prevail on any of the Esquimaux to accompany us as guides, they left us here, and I sent back John Folster and Ouligbuck to take care of the property left behind.

Our course was nearly N.N.W., but a gale of head wind impeded our progress greatly. The temperature of the air was 52°; water of lake 40°. A few hours' poling, pulling, and tracking brought us to the end of the lake, which is about six miles long, from two hundred yards to half a mile broad, and in some places thirty fathoms deep. The lake, as well as the stream up which we had come, was named after our boat. We now turned to the westward and entered a narrow passage one-and-a-half miles long, which connects the lake we had passed through with the next one; the current was strong, but between poling and tracking we soon got into still water. Our course now turned again to the N.N.W., and after proceeding a mile in this direction, we put on shore for the night in a small bay, where we found a good supply of a plant *(andromeda tetragona)*, which answers very well for fuel.

28th. We did not get under weigh this morning until 6 A.M. as the men had a hard day's work yesterday, and did not get to rest until a late hour. The lake continues to trend in the same direction as before, but the banks are neither so high nor so rocky, being covered with short grass in many places instead of moss. The wind still kept ahead, so that it was past ten in the morning before we arrived at a portage, and while two of the men were preparing breakfast, the others were employed carrying over some of the baggage. This portage, which I named after Flett, one of the steersmen, was half a mile long; and being in some places soft and in others stony, it was half-past four before we were afloat in the lake on the other side of it. It being calm, great numbers of fish were seen in this small body of water, which was narrow and only two-and-a-half miles long, with a deep bay on each side, which gave it the form of a T. It received the name of Corrigal, after one of my men. We lost our way here for a short time, having entered a wrong arm of

the lake.   At 8 P.M. we arrived at another portage, which being a short one was soon got over.
We pulled in a N. W. direction across this lake for
about three miles to a shallow streamlet that flows
from it; here we were to make our third and I
hoped our last portage.   We left this for our next
morning's work, as it was now half-past 10 P.M.
There was a great number of stones set up here
for the purpose of frightening the deer into the
water.   A large white wolf was seen.

The morning of the 29th was raw and cold, with
a gale of wind from N.W. by N.   We got over the
portage (which, although short, was covered with
rough granite stones that stuck to our boat's iron-
shod keel like glue) at 20 minutes after 6, and
embarked on what I then supposed was another
lake, but which afterwards turned out to be a portion of the second lake we had entered, and the
largest body of fresh water we had yet seen.   I
named it after my much-respected and kind friend,
Alexander Christie, Esq., Governor of Red River
Colony, whose name has been so often favourably
mentioned by Arctic travellers.

After pulling W.N.W. for eight miles, we were
again in doubt about the route, and whilst on my
way to some high ground in order to ascertain it, I
shot a fine buck with an inch and a half of fat on
his haunches.

We advanced two miles to the head of a small
inlet, whence I set out with one of the men to a

neighbouring rising ground to endeavour to obtain a view of our future route, and, if possible, to get a sight of the sea. After a fatiguing walk over hill and dale, our eyes were gladdened with a sight of what we so anxiously looked for, but the view was far from flattering to our hopes. The sea, or rather the ice on its surface, was seen apparently not more than twelve miles distant, bearing north; but there was not a pool of open water visible. It was evident that our detention in the lakes had as yet lost us nothing. Returning at 8 P.M., I sent four men in two parties to endeavour to discover the best route, one party being ordered to trace a considerable lake in a N.N.W. direction, and, if possible, discover its outlet.

30th. — The men sent off last night returned between 1 and 2 this morning: those who went to the N.W. reported that there was a small stream flowing towards the Arctic Sea from the farthest extremity of the lake they had traced.

As this account agreed with what we had heard from the Esquimaux, there was no doubt that we were now in the right track. We had to cross two portages, each a quarter of a mile, and traverse a lakelet one mile in extent, before we reached the body of water which the men had traced to its outlet. It was half-past 2 before we accomplished this work, there being many obstructions in the form of large granite stones, among and over which we had to drag the boat.

The lake in which we now found ourselves is upwards of 27 fathoms deep, about 6½ miles long, and not more than half a mile broad; it lies nearly N. by W., and is bounded by banks much more steep and rugged than any we had yet passed, being in some places two or three hundred feet high. It is situated in latitude 66° 55′ N., and longitude 87° 35′ W. We found that the longest and most difficult portage was now before us. By the time we had the baggage carried half way over it was getting late, and we did not take dinner until 9 p.m.

The following morning was cloudy, with a cold north breeze, which was not at all unfavourable for the work we had to do. We went to work at an early hour, but our advance was very slow, as the portage fully realised the bad opinion that we had formed of it. Hitherto, by laying the anchor out some distance ahead, and having a block attached to the bow of the boat by a strop, or what sailors call a swifter, passing round her, we could form a purchase sufficiently strong to move her with facility, but here our utmost exertions were required, and the tracking line was frequently broken. A piece of iron an eighth of an inch thick, which lined the keel from stem to stern, was actually drawn out and doubled up, so that it was necessary to remove the whole. At half-past 10, when half-way across, we breakfasted, after which we met with a bank of snow, over which we went at a great rate. The latitude, 66° 59′ 37″ N., was observed. Near the extremity of the portage there were some ponds of water deep enough to float the boat, that helped us not a little. The descent of a steep bank fully a hundred feet high brought us into another fine lake eight miles long and one mile broad, lying nearly north and south, with steep rocky shores on its west side : the place where we came upon its waters was about three miles from its southern extremity. This lake was named "Miles," after a friend. As it was quite calm, we pulled up due north and entered a narrow inlet, out of which there was no passage. We had passed at a mile and a half from this a stream flowing from the lake, but it looked so insignificant that I could not suppose it to be the same that the Esquimaux had reported as having sufficient water for floating the boat. It was now too late, however, to look for any other exit, and we all betook ourselves to rest after a hearty supper, for which the fatigues of the day gave us an excellent appetite. Some of the men had large pieces of the skin stripped from their backs whilst lifting the boat over the various obstructions on the portage.

1st August.—Finding that there was no likelihood of there being any other outlet to the lake than the one we had seen, we took out the cargo, and hauling our boat over a shallow part, we reloaded and soon entered a narrow lake, the waters of which were very muddy. At half an hour before noon we landed to have breakfast, and the latitude 67° 4′ 22″ N., variation of the compass 66° 38′ W., were observed. The shores of this lake, being covered with a rich pasturage and a great variety of flowers, afforded a pleasing contrast to the country we had hitherto travelled through. There were great numbers of marmots here, with a well-beaten path leading from one burrow to another. After dragging the boat over many shallows, we arrived a little after 5 P.M. at high-water mark, in latitude 67° 13′ N., longitude 87° 30′ W. The tide being out, and there not being sufficient water to float the boat, I decided on remaining here until the flood made.

The recent foot-tracks of two Esquimaux were seen on the sand.

A short distance below where we stopped, the stream we had descended empties its waters into a small river which flows from the westward.

2nd. — As the tide did not rise so high by two feet during the night as it had done the previous day, the boat did not float; we were, consequently, obliged to carry our baggage a mile further down the stream, and afterwards, with much trouble, haul our boat over numerous shoals. We were now afloat in a salt-water lake, and on passing a small point two Esquimaux tents came in view. Not having got breakfast, I landed with the interpreter, and, whilst the men were cooking, went to ascertain if there were any inhabitants. All was quiet inside, but after calling once or twice outside the door of one of the tents, an old woman made her appearance, apparently just out of bed, as she was very coolly drawing on her capacious boots, whilst she surveyed her visitors without showing the slightest symptoms of alarm, although I afterwards learned that I was the first European she had ever seen. An old man soon after popped out his head alongside that of his better half, who appeared to be endowed with a flow of language which set all his efforts to say anything at defiance. A few trifling presents put us all, in a few minutes, on a most friendly footing. Their report of the state of the ice in the large bay before us was far from encouraging; they said that there was seldom sufficient water for the passage of one of their small canoes, and present appearances led me to suppose that they were correct. The name of the man was I-il-lak, of the woman Rei-lu-ak. The remainder of the party, consisting of their two sons and their wives, had gone a day's journey inland to hunt the musk-ox. From a chart drawn by the woman, who, as is usual, (at least among the Esquimaux) was much the more intelligent of the two, I was led to infer that there was no opening leading into the large bay but through the Strait of the Fury and Hecla, and Prince Regent's Inlet.

As soon as breakfast was over, in which our new friends joined us, we crossed the lake, which is 6 miles long by $1\frac{1}{2}$ broad, and put on shore three of the men (W. Adamson, H. Mineau, and Nibitabo) who had assisted us across, and were now to walk back to Repulse Bay, a distance of forty-three miles. By them I sent orders to John Folster (the man left in charge) to make every possible preparation for wintering, and to keep up a friendly intercourse with the natives. My crew now consisted of George Flett, John Corrigal, Richard Turner, Edward Hutchison, Peter Mathieson, Jacques St. Germain, and William Ouligbuck. We now passed for two miles through a narrow channel—not more than 40 yards wide—among pieces of ice which were carried along with great rapidity by the ebb tide that had just commenced; this led us into the deep inlet which we had seen on the 29th ult. This inlet I named after Donald Ross, Esq., Chief-Factor. We found but little open water; by keeping near the rocks, however, we made some progress northward by using our ice-poles, and after advancing a mile or two I went upon a piece of ice and obtained the latitude 67° 15′ N. by a meridian observation of the sun in quicksilver. About eight miles to the north of this we passed a rocky point, which was named after Chief-Factor Hargrave, the gentleman in charge of York Factory when the expedition was fitted out, and who afforded every possible assistance towards its proper equipment. This point is formed of granite and gneiss, and has a very rugged appearance, there being neither moss nor grass on the rocks to soften their asperities.

At 7 A.M. on the 3rd, when a few miles past Point Hargrave, being completely stopped by ice, we put ashore and found a large wooden sledge, which we cut up for fuel. The wood was evidently the planks of some vessel (probably of the Fury or Sir John Ross's steamer the Victory) as there were holes in it bored with an auger. After working our way a mile or two further, we arrived at a high rocky cape having three elevations upon it lying east and west from each other. This head-land, which was honoured with the name of the lady of Sir John H. Pelly, Bart., Governor of the Hudson's Bay Company, is situated in latitude 67° 28′ N.; longitude by account 87° 40′ W.; variation of the compass 82° 36′ W.

It was low water to-day at 11 A.M., the fall of the tide being $8\frac{1}{2}$ feet, and the depth of water within a hundred yards of the beach from 3 to 5 fathoms, on a bottom of mud or sand.

Shortly after noon a fog came on so thick that we could only see a few yards round us; we, how-ever, pushed our way for $2\frac{1}{2}$ miles beyond Cape Lady Pelly, along a flat coast lined with mud banks from eight to ten feet high, frozen solid within a foot of the surface. At 4 P.M. the ice was too closely packed to allow us to proceed; we there-fore turned towards the shore, and after some trouble effected a landing. The fog still continued so thick, that, after wandering about for a few miles, I had much difficulty in finding the boat again, hid

E 2

52

as it was by the surrounding masses of ice. We were much at a loss for drinkable water, there not being a drop in the neighbourhood but what resembled chocolate in appearance.

In the forenoon some wolves, part of a band that had serenaded us last night with their dismal howlings, were seen prowling about; and a white-winged silvery gull (*L. leucopterus*), a diminutive sandpiper (*tringa minuta*), and a marmot were shot.

4th.—There was a drizzling rain with thick fog all night, but not a breath of wind. As the tide flowed the ice moved slowly and silently round us, so that in the morning we had not more than a yard or two of open water near us, being blocked in on all sides by pieces from 15 to 20 feet thick. The rise of the tide was not less than nine feet. In the forenoon I walked upwards of five miles along the shore to the north-westward, passing a few low sandy points about a mile and a half from each other, which formed a succession of small bays, into each of which a ravine with high and steep mud banks opened, down which a streamlet of pea-soup-coloured water flowed. We fell in with the heads and horns of several musk cattle and reindeer, and saw recent footmarks of some of the latter, but they had probably been driven some distance away by the wolves we saw yesterday. Marmots were numerous in every direction, chattering to each other, and rising on their hind legs to obtain a better view of the strangers. Many golden plovers and different kinds of sandpipers were flying about, and a jager (*L. parasiticus*) was shot: some plants were also collected. The travelling along this coast was extremely fatiguing, being very often nearly knee-deep in a very adhesive mud.

The thermometer rose as high as 70° in the forenoon; in the afternoon it fell to 48°; and in the evening the weather was cold and unpleasant, with heavy rain.

5th.—During the greater part of last night the rain continued, but it was perfectly calm, although by the lead of the clouds we were in hopes of a breeze of wind off shore. Our boat being in danger of injury from some heavy masses of ice that were turning over near us, we moved a dozen yards nearer the land. Our new situation, however, was little better than the one we had left, for as soon as the tide began to ebb large pieces of our "enemy" broke away and fell with a loud crash close alongside of us. It was high-water this morning at 3 o'clock, the rise of the tide being 11 feet 6 inches, whilst that of yesterday evening was only 5½ feet, an irregularity resembling that which was observed by Captain Sir J. Ross on the shores of Boothia. The temperature of the air in the morning was 46°, but rose to 65° during the day, which was very hazy, with occasional showers and a fresh breeze off shore; but this had not the slightest effect upon the ice, and led me to believe that the Esquimaux report as to the navigation being always obstructed here is correct.

Seeing that there was no probability of our getting

along shore towards Dease and Simpson's farthest,
I determined to retrace our route, and if possible
cross over to Melville Peninsula for the purpose
of surveying its western shore, towards the Strait
of the Fury and Hecla.

In the evening, when the tide, which on the present occasion rose only 4½ feet, was in, we endeavoured to extricate ourselves; and after some hours
of hard labour in chopping off some points of ice,
and pushing aside such pieces as were not aground,
we got a few hundred yards from the beach, and
into water a little more open.

About half-past ten a young buck was observed
on a piece of ice half-a-mile to seaward, having been
forced to take the water to avoid some wolves, one or
two of which were seen skulking along shore watching
for the return of the animal. The state of our larder
did not permit us to be merciful, so the poor deer
had little chance of escape from his biped and qua-
druped enemies when acting in concert. After a
long chase he was shot whilst swimming from one
floe to another. Having pulled and poled along
shore all night, we landed for breakfast at 8 h. 30 m.
A.M., on the 6th, about three miles to the south of
Point Hargrave. The continued rain and fog had
so completely saturated everything with damp that
we had not a dry stitch of clothes to put on, and
our bedding and fuel were in the same state; fortunately the weather was mild, so that we did not feel
much inconvenience from this.

Finding that the ice was clearing away a little—

the effect of a south-east wind,—we directed our course towards the nearest point of Melville Peninsula, which bore east (true) of us, distant ten miles, and after threading our way among much heavy and close-packed floes, which obliged us to make frequent and long detours, after five hours' hard work we reached the land during a thunder-storm accompanied by torrents of rain.

Our landing place was a long rocky point having a deep ice-filled inlet on its south side. To this point I gave the name of Cape Thomas Simpson, after the late enterprising traveller of that name.

As we could not proceed on account of the thick fog and the state of the ice, we secured the boat to the rocks, and the men although drenched to the skin went immediately to sleep, eighteen hours of hard work at the oars and ice-poles having thoroughly tired them all.

During the night of the 6th the weather was thick with occasional rain, but about 6 in the morning of the 7th a fresh breeze from the south-east dispersed the fog. As soon as it was cleared up we renewed our voyage, but our progress was very slow, having our old opponent to contend with ; in four hours we gained as many miles and were again stopped. Seeing some deer near the beach, we landed, and whilst two of us had a fruitless chase after them the remainder of the party were busy cooking and drying our clothes, blankets, &c. The temperature of the air was 52°, that of the water 35°.

The breeze gradually increased as the day advanced, and went round to the east, which drove the ice a short distance from the shore. We embarked again between 9 and 10 A.M., and ran to the eastward for a league or more, when the breeze having changed into a heavy gale, our boat ran great risk of being injured by the ice, of which we found it impossible to keep altogether clear. We therefore pulled up to a number of grounded pieces (a line of which completely barred us from the shore), and made fast to the largest of them. In getting this far we were in much danger from the falling, or breaking off, of overhanging masses (some of them 20 feet in height), which were crashing all around us, and under which we had frequently to pass. At 5 A.M. our floe got afloat, and began driving to leeward at a great rate. We just got the boat clear in time to prevent its being crushed against a berg that still remained fast. Some of the smaller pieces lying between us and the land having now floated, we managed to clear a passage for ourselves; yet although we had only a quarter of a mile to go, so strong was the gale that it required the utmost exertions of six men at the oars to reach the shore, when, having secured the boat and raised an oilcloth to keep off the rain, which had again commenced, we had our supper of pemmican and water, and retired to bed for the night.

8th.—On getting up this morning I found that it had become quite calm, and that the ice was coming in so thick and fast with the flood tide, that we had to move from our position as fast as possible. On pushing out to sea it soon became apparent that we could not proceed on our course, and that there was but little open water in the direction from whence we had come, and even that was fast filling up. As we could neither advance nor remain in safety where we were, there was only one course open to us, and that was to return towards the place from which we had started.

It was now evident that this large bay was completely full of ice; for had this not been the case, the gale of yesterday must have cleared the coast for many miles. It was with a sad heart that I turned the head of our boat towards our starting point, where I purposed to await some favourable change in the state of the ice, and at the same time learn how the people left at Repulse Bay were getting on with preparations for wintering, which now appeared inevitable. The weather continued so much overcast that no observations could be obtained. In the afternoon a light breeze sprang up from W.N.W., which enabled us to reach in a short time Ross Inlet, where we had some trouble in finding the entrance of the river on account of the altered appearance of the rocks, it being now nearly low water and the shore clear of ice, compared with what it formerly was. We had much difficulty in towing up to the Salt Lake before mentioned, as the narrow but deep channel which led to it was, at this state of the tide, one continued rapid, and so strong was the force of the stream that our tracking line broke. We were soon snug in the Salt Lake, but had not been more than half an hour under shelter before almost every spot of open water outside was filled with ice, so rapidly had it followed in our wake.

When we arrived opposite the tents of our Esquimaux friends, they came running down to the beach led on by the old lady whose fluency of speech I have already remarked, and who appeared determined to sustain her character on this occasion by making more noise than all the others put together, and expressing her joy at our return by loud shouts. The old people had during our absence been joined by the musk-ox hunters, two fine young active-looking fellows (named Ark-shuk and I-vit-chuck) and their wives. These women were the cleanest and best-looking I had yet seen. They were tatooed much in the same way as those at Repulse Bay. The hunters said they had been unsuccessful, but as each of the women had the tail, or a portion of the shaggy hair of the neck, of a musk-ox in her hand as a musquito flapper, their veracity was rather doubted. There was only one child with them, a sickly-looking boy of six or seven years, stepson to a man named Shi-shak, who arrived about an hour after us in his kayak from an unprofitable walrus hunt.

I learnt from our Esquimaux acquaintances that the deer had commenced migrating southward.

This being the case, I prepared to walk across to
Repulse Bay to see what progress the party left
there had made in their work. The weather had
been so cloudy for the last week that no observations
of any value could be obtained.

Leaving three men and Ouligbuck's son in charge
of the boat, I started at 6.30 A.M. on the 9th, in company with Corrigal, N. Germain, and Matheson, to
cross the isthmus, taking a S.S.E. direction; but it
was impossible to keep this course for any great
distance, as we were forced to make long circuits to
avoid precipices and arms of lakes. After a most
fatiguing day's march over hill and dale, through
swamp and stream, we halted at half-past 6 P.M.
close to the second portage crossed on our outward
route. To gain a distance of twenty miles we had
travelled not less than thirty. Our supper was soon
finished, as it was neither luxurious nor required
much cooking, consisting of our staple commodities
pemmican " cold with water."

10th.—The morning was raw and cold with some
hoar frost, and there not being a blanket among the
party and only two coats, our sleep was neither
long, sound, nor refreshing. In fact I had carried
no coat with me except a thin Macintosh, which,
being damp from the rain of yesterday, had become
an excellent conductor of caloric, and added to the
chilly feeling instead of keeping it off.

There is one advantage in an uncomfortable bed;
it induces early rising, and it proved so in the pre-

sent instance, for we had finished breakfast and resumed our journey by half-past 2 A.M. The travelling was as difficult as that of yesterday, but we had the advantage of a cool morning and got on more easily. At 7 o'clock we arrived at the narrows which separate Christie and North Pole Lakes, where we found the greater number of the Esquimaux we had seen, encamped, waiting for deer crossing over. Some of them immediately got into their kayaks and paddled across to our side of the lake, but with so much caution that it was evident we had not yet wholly gained their confidence.

At 2 P.M. we arrived at Repulse Bay with most enviable appetites, but rather foot-sore, our shoes and socks having been entirely worn through long before we reached our destination.

CHAPTER IV.

ON our arrival at Repulse Bay we found the men all well, but getting no more fish and venison than was barely sufficient to support them. Having taken but a scanty breakfast, I fully enjoyed my dinner here, but I reversed the usual order of

62

eating the same, taking my venison steak first (it being soonest cooked), and salmon as second course.

This was to me the most anxious period during the expedition; nor will this appear strange when I mention that it was necessary to decide, and that promptly, on one of two modes of proceeding, namely, whether to leave the whole survey to be completed during the following spring and summer, or to endeavour to follow it up this autumn. After mature consideration I determined on adopting the first of these measures, and giving up all hopes of prosecuting the survey at present.

My reasons for arriving at this conclusion I shall briefly mention, as such a step may appear rather premature. I saw from the state of the ice and the prevalence of northerly winds that there was no probability of completing the whole of the proposed survey this season; and although part of the coast, either towards the Strait of Fury and Hecla, or towards Dease and Simpson's farthest, might be traced, yet to accomplish even this might detain us so long that there would be no time to make the necessary preparations for wintering, and we should thus be under the necessity of returning to Churchill without accomplishing the object of the expedition, or, if we remained at Repulse Bay, run the risk of starving, for I could obtain no promise of supplies from the natives, and all the provisions we had carried with us would not go far to support the party throughout the winter. We should thus have to depend almost, if not altogether, upon our own exertions for the means of existence both in regard to food and fuel.

It ought to be borne in mind that we were differently situated from any party that had hitherto gone to these cold and barren regions. The resources of the country were quite unknown to us; it was not likely that the deer would remain near at hand all winter, as we were at too great a distance from the woods; and it was very evident, for the same reason, that we should not be able to procure any sort of fuel after the first fall of snow, which there was little doubt would occur some time in September.

Before reaching the Arctic Sea to the west of Melville Peninsula, I was for various reasons inclined to agree with the opinion of Sir John Ross, " that Boothia was part of the continent of America." This opinion was strengthened when I observed the great rise and fall of the tide, which must have affected the tides at the Castor and Pollux River, had there been a strait of any width separating Boothia from the mainland, unless indeed the assumption of Captain Sir J. Ross, that " the sea to the west of Boothia stands at a higher level than that on the east side," be correct. In that case there would be a continual easterly current, which could scarcely fail to have been noticed by so acute an observer as Simpson.

Retaining one man with myself to guard our

64

stores and attend the nets, on the 11th I sent over the remaining six to assist in bringing over the boat. Ouligbuck had now been about two days looking for deer, and I began to feel anxious about him, when he made his appearance between 9 and 10 A.M. with the venison of a young deer on his back.

As soon as my companion had returned from the nets, out of which he got no fish, I took a walk for the purpose of looking out for fishing stations and a site for our winter house. For the latter I could find no better place than a narrow but not deep valley within a few hundred yards of our landing-place, and about a hundred and fifty from North Pole River on its east side. There appeared to be various small bays along shore to the eastward which were likely to produce fish. A flock of laughing geese (*anser albifrons*) flew past quite close to me; but having only my rifle, I could but send a ball after them and missed as was to be expected.

In a small pond an eider-duck was observed with her young brood apparently not more than twelve days old. The male eider and king ducks had already left this quarter, having migrated to the southward.

12th.—A cloudy day with a strong breeze from N.N.W. Two salmon and a trout were got from the nets, but Ouligbuck killed no deer. In the evening, when on my way to set a net in a lake at no great distance, I fell in with a covey of ptarmigan, (*T. rupestris,*) most of the young being strong on the wing, and bagged eighteen brace in an hour or two. Knocking down those birds on this day made me half fancy myself among the grouse in my own barren native hills.

On the 13th the weather was raw and cold with frequent showers, and a gale of wind from the same quarter as the day before. Four salmon were caught, and a deer was shot. The thermometer varied from 36° to 38°. Four Esquimaux men and two women visited us to-day.

The 14th was much like the 13th, but there was no rain. As the visits of the natives had now become rather frequent, and as they brought nothing with them, but appeared to expect both food and presents, I bade Ouligbuck say that we could not afford to feed them any longer, and that they had better return to their huts, where I knew they were killing deer enough to support themselves. On returning from my daily walk, I found that our friends had taken leave rather hurriedly, having been detected appropriating some salt fish, which they could not eat. For this they were sharply reprimanded by the interpreter, and one of the ladies was most ungallantly accused by her husband of being the offender. Corrigal and I hauled the seine in the evening and caught thirty-three salmon; fourteen more were got out of the nets.

15th.—This was a beautiful day throughout. In

F

the evening, the sky being clear and cloudless, some stars were visible, and a few streaks of orange-coloured aurora showed themselves to the southward. The seine was again hauled, and thirty-two salmon (some of them very small) caught, whilst the nets produced eleven more. Just as we were landing our fish, the men who had been taking over the boat made their appearance, being a day earlier than I expected. By keeping the proper route three of the portages were avoided, and they had the advantage of a fine fair breeze all through the lakes. The large bay (Akkoolee) was reported as being more closely packed with ice than before. This was nothing but what I should have expected after the late north-westerly winds.

The two Esquimaux, Arkshuk and Ivitchuck, ("Anglice" Aurora and Walrus,) who had been engaged to aid in dragging the boat over the portages, had wrought well, and readily accommodated themselves to the habits of the men. They were well recompensed; and Ivitchuk (a merry little fellow) was engaged to accompany me on my intended spring journeys.

The boat was for the present left at North Pole Lake, as it might still be required there.

The 16th was a day of rest, and the 17th was so stormy and wet that little work could be done.

All hands were now busily employed making preparations for a long and dreary winter; for this purpose four men were set to work to collect stones for building a house, whilst the others were occu-pied in setting nets, hunting deer, and gathering fuel. Our work was much impeded by rainy weather, particularly the house building, as the clay or mud was washed away as soon as applied.

We found that our nets were so much cut up by a small marine insect from a half to three-quarters of an inch long, resembling a shrimp in miniature—the favourite food of the salmon—that it was quite impossible to keep them in repair. I thought to destroy their taste for hemp by steeping the nets in a strong decoction of tobacco, but it had no effect.

On the 2nd September our house was finished; its internal dimensions were 20 feet long by 14 feet broad, height in front $7\frac{1}{2}$ feet, sloping to $5\frac{1}{2}$ at the back. We formed a very good roof by using the oars and masts of our boats as rafters, and covering them with oilcloth and moose skin, the latter being fixed to the lower or inside of the rafters, whilst the former was placed on the outside to run off the rain. The door was made of parchment deer-skins stretched over a frame of wood. The walls were fully two feet thick, with three small openings, in which a like number of windows, each having two panes of glass, were placed.

Our establishment was dignified with the name of Fort Hope, and was situated in 66° 32′ 16″ N.; longi-tude (by a number of sets of lunar distances with objects on both sides of the moon) 86° 55′ 51″ W.

68

The variation of the compass on 30th August was
62° 50′ 30″ W.; mean dip of the needle, and the
mean twice of a hundred vertical vibrations in the
lide of declination 226″.

A sort of room was formed at one end by putting
up a partition of oilcloth. In this, besides its
serving as my quarters, all our pemmican and some
of the other stores were stowed away.

From the 5th to the 13th I was up at North Pole
and Christie Lakes in the boat with three men, our
object being to look out for fishing stations, and
also to purchase dogs from the Esquimaux. The
wind being from the north, we did not reach the
Esquimaux encampment till the 10th. They had
shifted their tents from the narrows to a small point
about eight miles up Christie Lake, where the deer
were more numerous, among which they seemed
to have made great havoc, to judge by the abundance of skins and venison lying in all directions.
Our friends were delighted to see us, and had
improved much in appearance, the only poor animals
about them being their dogs, which appeared to get
no more to eat than was barely sufficient to keep
them in life. I looked out four of the best, being
all I wanted at present, for which I promised a
dagger each, intending to take them with us on our
return. During our stay here a band of deer came
to the edge of the lake, and after feeding a short
time took the water. Three of the natives slipped
noiselessly into their kayaks, and lay waiting, until

the deer were far enough out in the water, to intercept them, but just as they were on the eve of starting the wind changed a little, and the deer smelling their enemy wheeled about, and were soon in safety on the beach from which they had started.

Many large flocks of Hutchins and snow geese had been seen for the last few days passing to the southward. The blue-winged goose of Edwards is by some ornithologists considered as the young of the last named bird in one of its stages towards maturity, but this opinion I believe to be erroneous, for the following reasons.

During a ten years' residence at Moose Factory, on the shores of Hudson's Bay, I had many opportunities, every spring and autumn, of observing both the snow and the blue-winged goose in their passage to and from their breeding places, the marshes near Moose being favourite feeding ground.

In spring both species are very nearly alike in size, the blue-winged goose, although shorter, being rather the heavier bird. In the autumn there are four distinct varieties, two of which exactly resemble in size and plumage those seen in the spring, whilst the others are much smaller, and differ much from these and from each other in their markings; the young of the snow goose being of a light grey colour, darkest on the head and upper part of the neck; whilst the young of the blue-winged goose is of a dark slate colour, approaching to black on the head and neck. Neither do the young separate

70

from the old, as has been asserted; for families may be seen feeding by themselves all over the marshes, the old bird keeping a sharp look-out, and giving timely warning to her brood of any approaching danger. In fact the Indian, who has thoroughly studied the habits of the bird, takes advantage of her affection for her young, and of their attachment to their parent, to make both his prey. Well knowing that the young are easily decoyed by imitating their call and by mock geese set up in the marsh, and that the old bird, although more shy, will follow them, he waits patiently until she comes within range; if he shoots her he is pretty sure to kill the greater part of the others, as they continue to fly over and around the place for some time after.

During the night of the 10th, when near the north end of the lake, we experienced one of the severest snow storms I ever witnessed. As we were sleeping on shore we never thought of putting up any sort of shelter; the consequence was that in the morning we were covered with snow to the depth of a foot. Our boat, which had been hauled up on the beach, was blown away from her fastenings, and carried several hundred yards into the lake among some stones. Being the only one of the party provided on the spot with Macintosh boots, it fell to my lot to wade out to the boat, throw overboard the ballast, lift her bows over the stones, and take a line to the shore; which, from having miscalculated the depth of the water, I found a more disagreeable

task than I had expected. Fortunately the boat
sustained no injury. It was now about 6 o'clock
in the morning of the 11th, and as the storm continued unabated we made a sort of tent of our sails.
In doing this the men got so wet and cold, from the
snow thawing on them, that they could not even
light their pipes.

In the afternoon the weather improved, and we
were able to scrape a little fuel together, with which
we cooked some salmon and boiled a kettle of tea,
which made us feel quite comfortable again. We
thus combined breakfast, dinner, and supper in
one meal.

The hares had already acquired their winter coat,
and the golden plovers and sandpipers had all disappeared, but some Lapland and snow-buntings and
the shore-lark were still to be seen.

A little after noon on the 13th the wind shifted
to the S.W., and we got under weigh to return home.
A couple of hours brought us to the Esquimaux,
where we stopped to take on board our dogs. A
young lad also came with us to carry some medicine
for the patriarch of the tribe, who was labouring
under various complaints peculiar to old age. We
arrived at North Pole River at 6 P.M., having had
a beautiful run all the way.

As we were not likely to require the boat on the
lakes again this season, she was hauled up and placed
in security for the winter. While at the lake we had
not been able to procure much more food than was

72

necessary for our own use, but this may in part have been attributable to the bad weather.

The storm of the 10th had been much felt at our house, and so great was its force that the boat left there was lifted a few yards by it, but received no injury. Much heavy ice was driven into the bay and lay heaped up all along the shore.

Our house was still far from comfortable, the clay being quite wet and producing a most unpleasant feeling of dampness,—far more disagreeable than a much lower temperature with dry weather.

Our time was now continually occupied in collecting fuel, (portions of which, as soon as it became dry, were built up into small heaps on the rocks near the house,) in fishing, and in shooting deer and partridges.

The routine of our day's work was as follows : in the morning we were up before day-light ; the men got their orders for the several duties they had to perform, which were principally carried on out of doors, and at which they set to work immediately after rolling up their bedding and taking breakfast. This meal usually consisted of boiled venison, the water with which it was cooked being converted into a very excellent soup by the addition of some deer's blood, and a handful or two of flour.

Our dinner, or rather supper, consisted of the same materials as our breakfast, and was taken about 4 or 5 o'clock ; after that, my time was employed in writing my journal or making calculations ; whilst the men

were busy improving themselves in reading, arith-
metic, &c., in which I assisted them as much as my
time would permit. Divine service was read every
Sunday when practicable.

On the 20th the pools of water were covered
with ice sufficiently strong to be walked upon, and on
the 28th some hooks were set under the ice on the
lakes for trout. During the latter part of the month
deer were very numerous. As many as seventeen
were shot on the 28th, and on the following day ten
more were got, seven of which were killed by myself within a few miles of the house. On the 29th
a considerable portion of the bay was frozen over,
and the seals were seen popping up their heads
every now and then through the ice to keep breath-
ing places open.

The weather during this month having been very
changeable and stormy, and unfavourable for observations of all kinds, the sextant had frequently
been exchanged for the rifle—a not unwelcome exchange to one addicted to field-sports " from his
youth upwards."

Our sporting book for the month showed that we
had been doing something towards laying in a stock
of provisions for winter ; 63 deer, 5 hares, one seal,
172 partridges, and 116 salmon and trout, had been
brought in.

October.—During the first part of this month
some of the men were employed in building a store
of snow for our provisions, and covering it with two

of the sails. On the 12th and three following days
there was one continued storm which drifted the
snow all round the house as high as the roof, and
on the night of the 15th would have choked all our
dogs that were chained outside, had not Adamson
and another got up and cut their fastenings. On
the 16th, when it cleared up, the thermometer first
fell to zero.

The cold had now penetrated in-doors and frozen
the clay on the walls, which made us much more comfortable. On attempting to open some books that
had been lying on a shelf, I was surprised to find
that the leaves were all frozen together ; when I
mention this, and also that our powder horns
and every other article that was bound with brass
or silver burst their fastenings, some idea may be
formed of the dampness of our house whilst the clay
on the walls was wet.

On the 19th, when out shooting, having killed
one deer, I went in pursuit of another (a large
buck) that had been wounded, and put four balls
through him. Thinking that the last ball had
settled the business, (for he had fallen,) I went
carelessly up to him without re-loading my rifle,
and when within a few yards I believe I apostro-
phized the animal much in the following strain—
" Ah! poor fellow, you are done for at last!"
when the deer, as if he had understood what I said,
and thought I was adding insult to injury, sprung
to his legs in a moment, and at a couple of bounds

his horns were within a foot of me. Circumstanced
as I was, I thought with Falstaff " that discretion
was the better part of valour," and beat a hasty
retreat, laughing heartily all the time at the strange
figure we must have made. Taking the deer by the
horns could have been of no use, and might have
cost me some troublesome bruises and scratches.

Twelve Esquimaux and a boy visited us on the
23rd; among whom was the man (named Shi-ma-kuk)
to whom the sledge belonged, part of which we had
used for fuel when near Cape Lady Pelly with the
boat. He was now rewarded, and apparently so
much to his satisfaction that he would have had no
objections to have another sledge burnt on the same
terms. They reported that the bay, to the west of
Melville Peninsula, had been packed full of ice ever
since we were over there, until a few days before
they came away, when there was some open water
to be seen. Besides purchasing five dozen rein-deer
tongues, a seal-skin full of oil, and some other articles, we added two good dogs to our team.

Among other information they told me that there
was an island in Akkoolee (the large bay west of
Melville Peninsula,) named Sha-took, (which means
low or flat,) on which large trees grew; but they
acknowledged that none of them had ever been on
the island, although they had been near enough to
see the trees distinctly. In this I believe their
imaginations had deceived them, aided perhaps in
some degree by a peculiar state of the atmosphere,

76

during which the appearance of the land has been
so distorted that it has been mistaken for woods.
Some round sticks, probably spars belonging to one
of the two vessels left in Prince Regent's Inlet,
having been picked up along the west shore of
Melville Peninsula, had no doubt strengthened the
opinion they had formed. Two of their party whom
we had never seen, were drowned in Miles Lake by
falling through the ice ; the one in chasing a deer,
and the other, it is supposed, in attempting to save
his companion.

Our visitors left us on the 25th, promising to
return soon with some deer-skin dresses. During
the whole of the month we were occupied much
the same way as in the previous one. Deer were
numerous during the first part of it, but scarce
latterly ; sixty-nine were shot, but the produce of
our nets had fallen very low, eighteen salmon and
four trout being all we caught. The highest temperature of the month was 38°, whilst the lowest was
15°. Although there was a great deal of very
stormy weather, there were some clear calm nights,
of which I took advantage to obtain lunar distances.

Two observatories had been built of snow, with a
pillar of ice in each (at the suggestion of Captain
Lefroy, R. A.), the one for the dip circle, the other
for an horizontally suspended needle to try the
effects of the aurora upon it.

So much snow had fallen that it lay four feet

deep on the roof of our meat store, and was near breaking the masts which supported it; so that we were obliged to raise its walls about a fathom to prevent such an occurrence in future.

On the 4th November, when out looking for deer a little before day-light in the morning, I observed a band of animals coming over a rising ground at a quick pace directly towards me. I at first supposed them to be deer, but on a nearer approach they proved to be wolves, seventeen in number. They continued to advance at full speed until within forty yards, when they formed a sort of half circle to leeward. Hoping to send a ball through one of them, I knelt down and took what I thought a sure aim at a large fellow that was nearest; unfortunately it was not yet broad day-light, and the rascals all kept end on to me, so that the ball merely cut off a line of hair and a piece of skin from his side. They apparently did not expect to meet with such a reception, for after looking at me a second or two they trotted off, no doubt as much disappointed at not making a breakfast of me as I was at missing my aim. Had they come to close quarters (which they sometimes do when pressed hard for food) I had a large and strong knife which would have proved a very efficient weapon. On my way home I shot three hares.

On the 5th two partridges were shot which very much resembled the tetrao saliceti, but which I suppose to be the T. mutus. The parasitæ found on them differed from those usually found on the willow grouse.

We began during this month to find that we could not afford fuel to dry our clothes; I therefore adopted the plan that a celebrated miser took to warm his food, by taking them under the blankets with me at night, and drying them by the heat of the body. This, it may be supposed, was not very agreeable, particularly when the weather became colder, for the moisture froze during the day on the blankets, which sparkled with hoar frost when I went to bed.

In the afternoon of the 9th we had one of the most severe snow storms that had yet been experienced, and I was much alarmed at the non-arrival of four men who had gone in the morning to examine some nets and set others in North Pole Lake eight miles from the house. Guns were fired to attract the attention of the party, who made their appearance at half-past 8 P.M., when we had given up all hopes of seeing them until the following day. They had been upwards of eight hours in coming as many miles, and were like walking pillars of snow when they came in. The four dogs they had with them were still missing, having run off with the sled as soon as they smelt the house. On the following day they were found entangled with one another, and the sled stuck fast against some rocks. One or two of the dogs were completely covered up with snow, but all safe.

About 2 P.M. on the 25th, two Esquimaux men and a boy, named Arkshuk (Aurora Borealis), Took-oo-lak (the falling stick), and Che-mik-tee (snuff), came to see us with deer-skin clothes, &c. for barter.

I had a good deal of conversation through the interpreters with Arkshuk, whom I found rather intelligent and communicative. It appears that the favourite food of these Esquimaux is musk-ox flesh; venison ranks next, and bear and walrus are pre-ferred to seal and fish. Their theory regarding the sun and moon is rather peculiar. It is said that many years ago, not long after the creation of the world, there was a mighty conjuror (Esquimaux of course), who gained so much power that at last he raised himself up into the heavens, taking with him his sister (a beautiful girl) and a fire. To the latter he added great quantities of fuel, which thus formed the sun. For some time he and his sister lived in great harmony, but at last they disagreed, and he, in addition to maltreating the lady in many ways, at last scorched one side of her face. She had suffered patiently all sorts of indignities, but the spoiling of her beauty was not to be borne; she therefore ran away from him and formed the moon, and continues so until this day. Her brother is still in chase of her, but although he sometimes gets near, he will never overtake her. When it is new moon, the burnt side of the face is towards us; when full moon, the reverse is the case.

The stars are supposed to be the spirits of the dead Esquimaux that have fixed themselves in the heavens, and falling stars, or meteors, and the aurora borealis, are those spirits moving from one place to another whilst visiting their friends.

The highest, lowest, and mean temperature of November were respectively $+ 28°$, $—25°$, and $+ 0.68$. Only twelve deer, nine hares, and a few partridges had been shot, whilst our nets produced about sixty fish, the greater part of which were small.

CHAPTER V.

Winter arrangements completed—Learn to build snow houses— Christmas-day—North-pole River frozen to the bottom—1st January — Cheerfulness of the men — Furious snow-storm — Observatories blown down—Boat buried under the snow— Ouligbuck caught in the storm—Dog attacked by a wolf— Party of natives take up their residence near Fort Hope— Esquimaux mentioned by Sir John Ross known to them—Boat dug out of the snow—A runaway wife—Deer begin to migrate northward—A wolf-chase—First deer of the season shot— Difficulty of deer-hunting in spring—Dimensions of an Esquimaux canoe – Serious accident to Ouligbuck—A conjuror— Preparations for the journey northward – Temperature—Aurora Borealis.

DURING December we completed our various buildings, and formed passages under the snow, so that we could without exposure go to any of them. There were four houses, viz. : one for provisions, another for fuel, a third for oil, dog's meat, &c., and a fourth for the men's spare luggage, for which there was no room in the dwelling-house, and which had been stowed in the tents until it was found necessary to take them down.

G

Being desirous of requiring as little assistance from the Esquimaux as possible, I attempted to build a snow house after the native fashion, and succeeded tolerably well; finding that the process was not so difficult as I anticipated, after a few trials one or two of the men became very good masons. We had now no encouragement to move much about, as there was no game to be seen, and the weather was very unsettled, and consequently no more exercise was taken than was necessary to keep us in good health. In stormy weather, not being able to get out of doors, the men wrestled or played some game which called the muscles into action, and thus kept up the animal heat.

On the 21st, the sun's lower limb rose about double his diameter above a rising ground to the southward, on a level with Fort Hope. On the 23rd and 24th, whilst looking out some good venison for our Christmas dinner, we examined our stock of such provisions, and found that we had not enough to last us until the return of the deer in spring; fortunately we had still a good supply of pemmican left.

Christmas-day was passed very agreeably, but the weather was so stormy and cold that only a very short game at foot-ball could be played. Short as it was, however, it was sufficiently amusing, for our faces were every moment getting frost-bitten either in one place or another, so as to require the continual application of the hand; and the rubbing, running about, and kicking the ball all at the same time, produced a very ludicrous effect.

Our dinner was composed of excellent venison and a plum-pudding, with a moderate allowance of brandy punch to drink a health to absent friends.

For some time past, washing the face had been rather an unpleasant operation, as any water that got among the hair froze upon it immediately. This is mentioned by Sir George Back as having occurred once to him at Fort Reliance, in 1833. On the 28th, North Pole River got frozen to the bottom, so that we were forced to go to a lake to the S.W. of Beacon Hill, about half a mile distant, for water.

The 1st of January was as beautiful a day as we could have wished to begin the new year with. There was a light air of wind, and the temperature varied from — 23° to — 26°. After a most excellent breakfast of fat venison steaks, all the party were occupied for some hours with a spirited game at foot-ball, at which there was much fun, the snow being so hard and slippery that several pairs of heels might be seen in the air at the same time.

My dinner consisted of part of a hare and rein-deer tongue, with a currant pudding as second course. The men's mess was much like my own, except that they had venison instead of hare. A small supply of brandy was served out, and on the whole I do not believe that a more happy company could have been found in America, large as it is. 'Tis true that an agreeable companion to join me in a glass of punch, to drink a health to absent friends, to speak of by-gone times and speculate on the future, might have made the evening pass more pleasantly, yet I was far from unhappy. To hear the merry joke, the hearty laugh, and lively song among my men, was of itself a source of much pleasure.

On the 7th the tracks of a few deer were unexpectedly seen within a few miles of the house; and on the following day the thermometer showed a temperature of — 47°, the lowest we experienced during the winter.

The 9th was a more disagreeable day than any we had yet had. A storm from the north with thick snow-drift, and a temperature of 72° below the freezing point, made it feel bitterly cold. Fortunately we had some days before made a house for our dogs, else they must have inevitably been frozen to death. Such was the force of the gale for two days that both observatories were completely demolished, and wherever the snow banks projected in the slightest degree above the surrounding level, they were worn away by the friction of the snow-drift as if cut with a knife.

The thermometer indoors varied from 29° to 40° below the freezing point; which would not have been unpleasant where there was a fire to warm the hands and feet, or even room to move about; but where there was neither the one nor the other, some few degrees more heat would have been preferable.

As we could not go for water we were forced to thaw snow, and take only one meal each day. My waistcoat after a week's wearing became so stiff from the condensation and freezing of my breath upon it, that I had much trouble to get it buttoned.

The gale did not subside until the 15th, when we were busily employed repairing the damages done by the wind and drift. As a great weight of snow had lodged upon our boat, we were afraid she might be injured by the pressure, and some of the men were employed to search for her, but there was some difference of opinion about her exact situation, and it was two days before she was found, after digging to the depth of eight feet.

A stick was set up at one end of the boat that there might be no difficulty in finding the place again.

One cause of discomfort to me was the great quantity of tobacco smoke in our low and confined house, it being sometimes so thick that no object could be seen at a couple of yards' distance. The whole party, with the exception of myself, were most inveterate smokers; indeed it was impossible to be awake for ten minutes during the night without hearing the sound of the flint and steel striking a light. Of course I might to a great extent have put a stop to this, but the poor fellows appeared to receive so much comfort from the use of the pipe, that it would have been cruelty to do so for the sake of saving myself a trifling inconvenience.

This month was so stormy that the most of our

time when we could get out of doors was passed in clearing away the snow that drifted about our doors and over the house, and in rebuilding and repairing. The boat, and also the stick that had been set up as a mark, were completely covered over. On the 18th Ouligbuck had gone out to hunt, and did not return till the 25th, after I had given up all hopes of ever seeing him again in life. It appeared that he had visited the Esquimaux at Christie Lake for the purpose of speaking to them about not having kept their promise regarding some oil that they said they would bring to us, and which they had omitted to do. He had been caught by the storm of the 18th before he reached his friends, and was obliged to build a snow hut, in which he passed the night comfortably enough. On the following morning, when it cleared up a little, he found that he was not more than two hundred yards from his destination, which the thickness of the weather on the previous day had prevented him from seeing.

One of the dogs we had lent this party to aid in drawing some provisions to the coast had a narrow escape from a wolf. Having broken loose she set out on her return home, when she was attacked by the wolf, and treated much in the same way that Tam O'Shanter's mare was by Cutty Sark, for

> " The wolf had caught her by the rump,
> And left poor Surie scarce a stump."

On the last day of January some Esquimaux, who

were to take up their quarters near us, arrived with part of their luggage and provisions, and built their snow house near the south side of Beacon Hill. This would have been the best situation for our establishment, as it was completely sheltered from the northerly gales, but we were too late in making the discovery.

I visited the Esquimaux on the 1st February, and found the old man, named Shishak, and his wife in their comfortable house, which was so warm that my waistcoat, which had been frozen quite stiff for some time past, actually thawed. It was not easy to learn any of the peculiarities of these people, as Ouligbuck was rather shy about describing their habits. Ouligbuck's son informed me that even in winter they strip off all their clothes before going to bed.

When taking a walk on the 3rd I passed near the Esquimaux, and found one of them repairing the runners of his sledge. The substance used was a mixture of moss chopped up fine, and snow soaked in water, lumps of which are firmly pressed on the sledge with the bare hand, and smoothed over so as to have an even surface. The process occupied the man nearly an hour, during the whole of which time he did not put his hands in his mitts, nor did he appear to feel the cold much, although the temperature was 30° below zero.

On the 4th Ouligbuck set his gun for a wolf that had been prowling about for the last few days. The usual mode is to fix the gun to two sticks with its muzzle pointed to a bait placed at the distance of fifteen or twenty yards, with a line attached to it, the other end of which is fastened to the trigger; but Ouligbuck's plan was quite different from this. He enclosed the gun in a small snow house, in such a manner that there was nothing visible but the bait, which was not more than a foot from the muzzle, so that the shot could scarcely miss the head of the animal. When Ouligbuck went to his gun next morning, he saw the track of the wolf, and followed it to the dog-kennel, in which he had comfortably taken up his quarters; he immediately took the brute by the tail and dragged him outside much against his will, when he was soon dispatched with an ice-chisel. This animal was very large, but in the last stage of starvation, with a severe arrow or gun-shot wound in one thigh. He measured 5 feet 9 inches from the nose to the tip of the tail, (length of tail 1 foot 7 inches,) and his height at the shoulder was 2 feet 8 inches.

On the 7th a man named Ak-kee-ou-lik, who had promised us four seal-skins of oil, arrived and said that he could only let us have one, because the bears had broken into his "cache" and devoured nearly all its contents. This story I did not believe at the time, and I afterwards found out that it was false. I felt a good deal annoyed at the man's not keeping his promise, because we had depended much upon this supply for fuel and light.

To save the former, we had during part of last month taken only one meal a-day, and discontinued the comfort of a cup of tea with our evening repast. Of oil, our stock was so small, that we had been forced to keep early and late hours, namely, lying occasionally fourteen hours in bed, as we found that to sit up in a house in which the temperature was some degrees below zero, without either light or fire, was not very pleasant. Fortunately we all enjoyed excellent health, and our few discomforts, instead of causing discontent, furnished us with subjects of merriment. For instance, Hutchison about this time had his knee frozen in bed, and I believe the poor fellow (who by-the-bye was the softest of the party) was afterwards very sorry for letting it be known, as he got so heartily laughed at for his effeminacy.

On the 9th, one of the Esquimaux women (wife of Keiktoo-oo) that came to see us, had a brass wheel 1½ or 2 inches in diameter fastened on her dress as an ornament. It was evidently part of some instrument, probably of some of those left by Sir John Ross at Victoria Harbour. I wished to purchase it, but she would not part with it.

15th. — Akkeeoulik brought over a large and heavy hoop of iron, which had been at one time round the rudder head, bowsprit end, or mast head of a vessel, as he said it had been taken off a large stick. I did not buy it from him, as he was in disgrace for having disappointed me about the oil. About 1 P.M. on the same day a number of the natives paid us a visit, among whom were Ec-vu-chi, I-vit-chuk, and Ou-too-ouniak, three of the most decent and best behaved of the party. They brought us a quantity of venison, of which they had still a large stock, and some of which they were now willing to dispose of, as they found that they had more than was requisite for their own consumption.

They had frequently seen Ooblooria, Ikmallik, and some of the other Esquimaux mentioned by Sir John Ross, and I also further learnt that the man with the wooden leg, named Tulluahiu, was dead, but how long since I could not discover.

The greater part of the men had been employed for the last fourteen days digging away the snow from the boat to relieve her from the pressure, as she was covered up to the depth of more than twelve feet. This was no easy task; however, we managed it in the following manner. Having cut a narrow opening through the snow down to the boat, we erected a tackle over it and hoisted up the loose snow, as it was removed with spades and axes. After excavating a space the full length of the boat, and clearing the snow out of it, the bow and stern were alternately raised, and the blocks of snow which were chopped from the top pushed underneath to prevent its sinking down again. In this way the men could work without exposure, and when the weather was stormy the hole was covered with a sail, so that the snow-drift could not interfere with our labours. We had yesterday got her close to the top of the snow roof, and to-day the weather being fine she was hauled out and found to be uninjured, except a small split in one of her thwarts caused by the great weight. She was now placed in a situation where there was no danger of her being again drifted over.

The Esquimaux left us on the 17th, having behaved themselves in the most exemplary manner. One of Akkeeoulik's wives (quite a young dame with a most interesting squint) took this opportunity of leaving her husband and putting herself under the care of her father Outoo-ouniak, the alleged cause of her dissatisfaction being that she did not get enough to eat. The disconsolate man followed the party for some distance in hopes of persuading the runaway to return, but without success.

Our fuel getting rather scarce, some of the men were sent to dig among the snow for moss and heather, and they usually got as much in a day as would cook one meal, but as the spring advanced, and the snow began to disappear, two men could procure as much as we required. When the men were taking a walk after divine service on the 21st, they saw the traces of five deer going northward.

On the 22nd Turner commenced making two sledges for our spring journeys. They were to be from 6 to 7 feet long, 17 inches broad, and 7 inches high. The only wood we had for this purpose was the battens with which the inside of our boats was lined, it being necessary to nail three of them together to form runners of the required height. A wolf was shot by Ouligbuck during the night within 10 yards of the door of the house, and six or eight more were seen at no great distance off in the morning.

23rd. When taking my usual exercise, I came upon a white owl feasting on a hare which it had killed after a severe struggle, to judge by the marks on the snow. Half of it was already eaten. Another wolf was shot on the 25th at a set gun, but there was nothing of him to be found in the morning except a little hair and blood, all the rest having been eaten or carried off by his companions. Some more deer tracks were seen going northward. On the 26th the height of Beacon Hill was found to be 238 feet above the level of the sea at half-flood.

Next day Nibitabo saw thirty deer and ten partridges, but only shot two of the latter. The former were in the middle of a large plain, and took good care to keep out of gun-shot, much to the annoyance of our deer-hunter, who is one of the keenest sportsmen I have ever met with.

There were two wolves wounded by Ouligbuck's gun last night, one of which he caught before breakfast. I went with him after the other in the forenoon, and got sight of him about three miles from the house. Although his shoulder was fractured, he gave us a long race before we ran him down, but at last we saw that he had begun to eat snow, a sure sign that he was getting fagged. When I came up with him, so tired was he that I was obliged to drive him on with the butt of my gun in order to get him nearer home before knocking him on the head. At last we were unable to make him move on by any means we could employ. Ferocity and cowardice, often if not always, go together. How different was the behaviour of this savage brute from that of the usually timid deer under similar circumstances. The wolf crouched down and would not even look at us, pull him about and use him as we might; whereas I never saw a deer that did not attempt to defend itself when brought to bay, however severely wounded it might be.

On the 1st March one of our sledges that had been finished was tried, and found to answer well.

The deer were now steadily migrating northward, some being seen every day, but there were none killed until the 11th, when one was shot by Nibitabo; it proved to be a doe with young, the fœtus being about the size of a rabbit. The sun had so much power that my blankets by being exposed to the air got completely dried, being the first time that they had been free from ice for three months.

Shortly after divine service on the 14th, Akkeeoulik, who had gone some days before to his father-in-law's to endeavour to reclaim his better half, returned with his lost treasure, one of the most lazy and dirty of the whole party, and a most arrant thief to boot. Two deer were shot on the

15th, and two more on the 18th. Deer-hunting had become very different from what it was in the autumn. The greater part of the hollows which favoured our approach in the latter season were now filled up with snow, which, from wasting away underneath, made so much noise under foot that in calm weather it was almost impossible to get within shot. The deer were besides continually moving about in the most zig-zag directions, and were so much startled at the report of a gun that it was evident they had been a good deal hunted during the winter.

On the 20th Nibitabo was affected with inflammation of the eyes, which was relieved by dropping laudanum into them. On the 26th we made a new water hole on the lake, when the ice was found to be 6 feet 10 inches thick. I measured the dimensions of an Esquimaux canoe, and found them as follows:—length 21 feet, breadth amidships 19 inches, and depth where the person sits $9\frac{1}{2}$ inches. The timbers are one-half or five-eighths of an inch square, and placed three inches apart near the centre of the canoe, but gradually increased to five inches at each end. The cross-bars are three-quarters of an inch thick and a foot from each other; these were morticed into gunwales $2\frac{1}{2}$ inches broad by half-an-inch thick, the whole being covered with seal skin in the usual manner. Altogether it was much more neatly finished and lighter

than any I had seen in Hudson's Straits; but the
natives here have not attained the same dexterity in
managing them, as they cannot turn their canoes
without assistance after being capsized.

On the 31st Ouligbuck, who had been absent all
night, came home at 1 P.M. very faint from the
effects of a severe wound he had received on the arm
by falling on a large dagger which he usually
carried. On cutting off his clothes I found that the
dagger had passed completely through the right
arm a couple of inches above the elbow joint.

In the evening Shimakuk, who is a conjuror,
came in, and as Ouligbuck wished to try the effect
of his charms on the injured part, I of course had
no objections. The whole process consisted in
putting some questions (the purport of which I
could not learn) to the patient in a very loud voice,
then muttering something in a very low tone, and
stopping occasionally to give two or three puffs of
the breath on the wounded arm. During these
proceedings the men could with difficulty keep
their gravity; nor could I blame them, for the scene
was irresistibly ludicrous.

I observed that one of the conjuror's dogs was
lame, or rather very weak in the legs, and on asking
him the cause, he said that it arose from having
eaten trout livers when young.

The latter part of the month of March was spent,
by the majority of the party, in making preparations
for our journey, over the ice and snow, to the north-

ward, it having been my intention to set out on the 1st April; but the accident to Ouligbuck prevented this, as I did not wish to leave him until I saw that his wound was in a fair way of healing. Ivitchuk, our intended companion, had not yet made his appearance.

On the 3rd April the thermometer rose above zero, for the first time since the 12th December.

As the aurora was seldom noticed after this date, I may here make a few remarks on this subject. It was often visible during the winter, and usually made its appearance first to the southward in the form of a faint yellow or straw-coloured arch, which gradually rose up towards the zenith. During our stay at Fort Hope I never witnessed a finer display of this strange phenomenon than I had done at York Factory, nor did it on any occasion affect the horizontal needle as I had seen it do during the previous winter there.

The Esquimaux, like the Indians, assert that the aurora produces a distinctly audible sound, and the generality of Orkneymen and Zetlanders maintain the same opinion, although for my own part I cannot say that I ever heard any sound from it. A fine display, particularly if the movements are rapid, is very often succeeded by stormy or snowy weather, but I have never been able to trace any coincidence between the direction of its motions, and that of the wind.

CHAPTER VI.

EVERYTHING having been for some days in readiness for our contemplated journey, I only awaited
the arrival of our Esquimaux ally Ivitchuk. He
made his appearance on the 4th April in company

H

with his wife, his father and brother, and their wives. I could have well dispensed with the presence of the party, excepting the man who was to go with us, as there were many things to be attended to. It is strange that throughout the winter, with one or two exceptions, the visits of these people have happened on Sundays. Our intended travelling companion having received a coat from one, inexpressibles from another, leggings from a third, &c., was soon completely dressed " à la voyageur," not certainly to the improvement of the outer man, but much to his own satisfaction. Ouligbuck's arm being now in a fair way of recovery, there was no cause of detention.

The party, consisting, besides myself, of George Flett, John Corrigal, William Adamson, Ouligbuck's son, and Ivitchuk, started early on the morning of the 5th. We were accompanied by two sledges, each drawn by four dogs, on which our luggage and provisions were stowed. Our stores consisted of three bags of pemmican, seventy reindeer tongues, one half-hundred weight of flour, some tea, chocolate, and sugar, and a little alcohol and oil for fuel. At first the weather was far from favourable for travelling, as there was a gale of wind with snow, but about 8 A.M. the sky cleared up, and the day became as fine as could have been wished. The sun shone forth with great brightness, surrounded by a halo of the most brilliant colours, with four parhelia that rivalled the sun himself. Our route was the same as that followed in the boat last autumn; but although the snow was hard-packed and not rough, our sledges were too heavy to allow us to travel quickly. Numerous bands of deer crossed our path, and enlivened the scene at the same time that they kept up the spirit of our dogs. Our latitude at noon, by an observation of the sun, was 66° 42′ N., variation of the compass 64° W. Between 7 and 8 P.M., both dogs and men being somewhat fatigued with their day's work, we stopped on the east side of Christie Lake to build our snow hut, which our Esquimaux friend was so long in completing on account of the bad state of the snow for building, that it was 11 o'clock before we got into our blankets. The situation of our encampment was in latitude 66° 49′ 30″ N., longitude 87° 20′ W.

6th. — We passed a comfortable night, and it was 6 o'clock in the morning before we were again on the march; three hours more brought us to the northern extremity of the lake, where we had left a bag of flour "en cache" the previous autumn. Two men who had accompanied us, for the purpose of taking the flour back to our winter quarters, returned from this place.

A little before noon we arrived at the snow hut of the two Esquimaux, Shimakuk and Kei-ik-too-oo, who, with their families, had been staying some time here angling trout. I had agreed with those people that they should build a large snow house for our accommodation, having expected to reach them at the end of our first day's journey. In this we were disappointed; but, as the contracting party had prepared a fine roomy dwelling for us, they received the stipulated price—a clasp knife. At noon, when still on the lake, the latitude 66° 58′ 16″ N. was observed.

Kei-ik-too-oo having come with us for a short distance, I proposed that he should get his sledge and dogs and accompany us for two days; this, for a dagger as a consideration, he gladly agreed to do, and immediately went off at a great rate to bring up his team. Being quite light he soon overtook us, and was not long in getting a heavy load on. I soon saw the advantage of his iced runners over the iron ones, and determined to have ours done in the same way on the first opportunity; on this account we stopped sooner than we would otherwise have done, having travelled sixteen geographical miles. We found a number of old Esquimaux houses, one of which we prepared for our use by clearing out the snow that had drifted into it. Whilst the two Esquimaux were icing the sledges, the remainder of the men were cooking and preparing our bed; the latter being a very simple process, merely requiring the snow to be well smoothed, and one or two hairy deer-skins laid over it to prevent the heat of the body from thawing the snow. The weather was fair all day, and except in the morning when the thermometer was — 16°, it was rather warm for walking. After we got into our lodgings a strong breeze sprung up with thick drift. Some of the party were slightly affected with snow-blindness.

7th. — The weather was gloomy and dark this morning, with the thermometer at + 5° when we started at half-past 3. Our sledges ran much easier since they had received a coating of ice on their runners, although they were not yet equal to Kei-ik-too-oo's. We followed the same route as that taken by the boat last autumn until 9 o'clock, when being two miles from the sea we struck across land towards Point Hargrave; at noon we were in latitude 67° 16′ 51″ N., variation of the compass 74° 30′ W. We found the snow much softer than it was on the lakes and river, and our progress was consequently much slower than in the first part of the day.

At 2 P.M. we arrived at a small lake, about four miles from Point Hargrave. As this was the only fresh-water lake we were likely to meet with for some time, I determined to stop for the purpose of renewing the icing on the sledges, which had been a good deal broken by the irregularities of the road. Notwithstanding that we had gone only eighteen miles our dogs were very tired, and I began to fear that they would not hold out so well as was expected. Our Esquimaux friend was to leave us the next day, and as his sledge was light he expected to reach his house the same day. This is a favourite resort of the musk-ox as soon as the snow disappears. The mode of killing these animals is the same as that described by Sir J. C. Ross as practised in Boothia Felix by the Esquimaux : being brought to bay with dogs, they are either shot with arrows or speared.

When we resumed our journey at 5 o'clock next morning, there was a strong breeze right ahead with thick drift, the temperature being + 6°. A walk of three miles brought us to the coast about a mile from Point Hargrave. There was a great deal of rough ice along the shore, which gave both men and dogs much hard work to drag the sledges over. It had now begun to snow, and the drift was so thick that we could not follow the smoothest route ; we consequently advanced but slowly, taking four hours to gain five and a half miles, which brought us to Cape Lady Pelly.

Since leaving Fort Hope, I had measured every foot of the ground we had passed over with a line, but now the increased difficulty of the route made it requisite that all hands should be employed in dragging the sledges. One of our best dogs became quite useless, and although unharnessed would not walk, so that rather than lose the poor animal, we dragged him on the snow several miles before reaching our intended encampment.

After passing Cape Lady Pelly the coast turns rather more to the westward. The weather continued very unfavourable all day, there being much snow-drift; we however advanced seven miles farther, and at 4 P.M. built our night's lodgings on the ice, a few hundred yards from the shore. In an hour and a half we were comfortably housed. Finding that our day's journeys were much shorter than I had anticipated, our allowance of food for supper was somewhat reduced. The thermometer in the evening stood at $+ 11°$. Our snow hut was situated in latitude 67° 35′ N., longitude 87° 51′ W. both by account.

After a sound night's rest we resumed our journey at 5 in the morning of the 9th. There was some snow falling, but the wind had decreased, and the temperature of the air was $+ 2°$. Our course was N.W. by W. for three miles, when we came to a low point formed of shingle and mud, with some rocky rising grounds a few miles inland. This point received the name of Swanston, after a friend. A short time before noon the sky cleared, and very satisfactory observations for latitude and variation of the compass were obtained, the former being 67° 40′ 53″ N., the latter 71° 30′ W. The dog that had been unharnessed the day before had become still weaker, and as I did not wish to leave him to the mercy of the wolves, he was shot. We offered some of his flesh to the other dogs, but there was only one of them that would eat it.

Having walked fourteen miles, we arrived at a small river 70 yards wide, and, although it was only half-past three, we commenced building our snow house. We here found a number of stones which allowed us to place " en cache" half a bag of pemmican, some flour, shoes, &c., for our homeward journey.

The river, which is called Ki-ting-nu-yak, was frozen
to the bottom, but in summer it is a favourable fishing station, both salmon and a small species of the
white fish being found. I did not see any of the
latter, but from the description given by the Esquimaux I have no doubt that they frequent this part
of the coast.

The evening was beautifully clear, and the thermometer fell to — 16°.

10th.—There was a thick haze this morning with
light variable airs of wind ; temperature 6° below
zero. By striking straight out from land for a mile
or two, we got upon somewhat smoother ice, and
consequently made more progress. We passed a
number of hills, not of any great elevation however,
and at noon we were opposite one named Wiachat,
fully 500 feet high, and some miles from the coast.
Here the latitude 67° 53′ 24″ was observed, and the
coast turned off to the westward, forming a point
which was named Cape Weynton. We now commenced crossing a bay 5 or 6 miles deep, and apparently 12 wide, which received the name of
Colvile, in honour of the Deputy Governor of the
Hudson's Bay Company. A mouse or lemming
crossed our path, and the dogs, although they appeared to be scarcely able to put one foot before
another, set off at full speed in chase, and before
any one could interfere to save it, the poor little
animal was quivering in the jaws of the foremost.

Being unable to reach the north side of Colvile

Bay, at 4 P.M. we took up our quarters on the ice in our usual snug lodgings, in latitude 68° 2′ N., longitude 88° 21′ W. A high hill bearing west of us, and distant eight miles, called Oo-me-we-yak by the natives, was named after the late John George M‘Tavish, Esq., Chief Factor. Several of our dogs had become very weak—so much so that during the latter part of the day's journey they did little or nothing, thus giving us all much additional work. They also required much more food to keep them in good condition, than the dogs generally used in the fur countries. We only walked sixteen miles this day ; and I may here remark that all the distances mentioned in this journal are given in geographical miles.

Our usual mode of preparing lodgings for the night was as follows :—As soon as we had selected a spot for our snow house, our Esquimaux, assisted by one or more of the men, commenced cutting out blocks of snow. When a sufficient number of these had been raised, the builder commenced his work, his assistants supplying him with the material. A good roomy dwelling was thus raised in an hour, if the snow was in a good state for building. Whilst our principal mason was thus occupied, another of the party was busy erecting a kitchen, which, although our cooking was none of the most delicate or extensive, was still a necessary addition to our establishment, had it been only to thaw snow. As soon as the snow hut was completed, our sledges were unloaded, and every thing eatable (including parchment skin and moose skin shoes, which had now become favourite articles with the dogs) taken inside. Our bed was next made, and by the time the snow was thawed or the water boiled, as the case might be, we were all ready for supper. When we used alcohol for fuel (as we usually did in stormy weather) no kitchen was required.

On the following morning we started about the usual hour, and directing our course nearly north, a walk of five miles brought us to the opposite side of Colvile Bay, which terminated in a long point covered with boulders of granite and debris of limestone, and having a number of stone marks set up on it. To this point the name of Beaufort was given, in honour of the gallant officer who, with so much advantage to his country and to nautical science, presides over the hydrographical department of the Admiralty.

Five miles farther we reached another low point called by the Esquimaux E-to-uke, but renamed by me Point Siveright. The coast, now turning slightly to the westward of north, continued in nearly a straight line during the rest of this day's march.

We were now tracing the shores of a considerable bay, as the land after taking a sudden bend to the eastward followed a south-east direction as far as visible. At 4 P.M. we stopped and built our snow hut; the day had been fine throughout, and the temperature in the evening was 16° below zero. The shores of the bay are very low, with the exception of a high bluff point bearing S.E. by E. 6½ miles (by trigonometrical measurement). The point was named Cape Barclay, in honour of the Secretary of the Hudson's Bay Company, and the bay was called after my much respected friend, George Keith, Esq., Chief-Factor.

Since passing Colvile Bay the coast had become much lower and more level, giving every indication of a lime-stone country. Being anxious to save our fuel as much as possible, we filled two small kettles and a bladder with snow and took them to bed with us, for the purpose of procuring water to drink— a plan which was frequently adopted afterwards. Our dogs had now become most ravenous; although they received what was considered a fair allowance of provisions, everything that came in their way, such as shoes, leather mitts, and even a worsted belt, was eaten, much to the annoyance of the owners and to the merriment of the rest of the party. We enjoyed a cold supper of pemmican and water;—as we could afford a hot meal only once a day, we preferred taking it in the morning.

12th.—Being informed by our Esquimaux companion that, by crossing over land in a north-west direction to a large bay which he had formerly visited, we should shorten our distance considerably,

I determined on adopting the plan proposed. Our kettles of snow were found rather cool companions, but there was a little water formed. The bladder having been either leaky, or not properly tied, gave me and my next neighbour a partial cold bath. The morning was delightful, being clear and calm, with a temperature of — 22°. We started at half-past 5, and after having walked a short distance came to some loose pieces of granite and limestone, which afforded an opportunity, not to be lost, for making a deposit of provisions for our return journey.

After tracing the shores of the bay for three miles and a half further north to latitude 68° 18' N., longitude by account 88° 26' W., we left the coast and proceeded over land in a north-north-west direction. Walking became more difficult, and the snow was too soft to support the sledges, the ice on the runners of which was now entirely worn off. A mile's walk brought us to a small river with high mud banks, and frozen to the bottom : it is named A-ma-took by the natives, and takes its rise from a lake of the same name about a day's journey west of us. We next passed between two elevations covered with limestone. I ascended that on the right-hand or to the east of us, it being the highest and having two columns of limestone, the one fourteen, the other nine feet high, at its western extremity. There were many places here denuded of snow, showing that the sun had already acquired great power. At noon we were in latitude 68° 22′ 19″ N., variation of the compass 79° 35′ W. An hour after, we reached a small lake, where we halted on account of our dogs being quite knocked up, although we had only advanced twelve miles; I therefore ordered a hut to be built that we might afford the dogs time to recruit, and also have the sledge-runners put in order. We found the ice on the lake 4 feet 8 inches thick, but we were disappointed to find that there were no fish to be caught. We here enjoyed water ad libitum, a luxury that had been rather sparingly dealt out for the last few days. Ivitchuk drank as much as would have satisfied an ox. The thermometer in the evening was 9° below zero. A few tracks of foxes were here seen, but no signs of deer or musk-oxen. This part of the country appeared miserably barren in every respect.

On the morning of the 13th we commenced our march at 2.30 A.M.; the weather was fine with light airs from the north-west: thermometer —15°. At 5 o'clock we passed a small lake about a mile and a half long, and an hour afterwards reached another of considerable size. Tung-a-lik, as the lake is called by the Esquimaux, is 7 miles long due north and south, and varying in breadth from a mile to a mile and a half. Near its centre was a curious-looking island, about 7 feet high and 200 yards in extent, covered with granite boulders and limestone. Its form is as nearly as possible that of a semicircle, the concavity being towards the south. To this lake I gave the name of Ballenden, after a much valued friend. When near the north end of Ballenden Lake (over which we had travelled rapidly, the snow being both hard and smooth), we turned more to the west. At noon we arrived at a lake which was to be our resting place for the night, as, although small, it was said to contain both trout and salmon; but, after cutting through five feet of ice, we did not succeed in catching any, although we tempted them with a bait from a buffalo hide. In the afternoon the weather became very gloomy; a strong breeze sprang up accompanied by a thick haze, and the thermometer rose to — 11°. By meridian observation our latitude was 68° 36′ 58″ N., variation of the compass 78° W., longitude by account 88° 49″ W.

14th.—This morning was so stormy, with thick drift and snow, that we could not start so early as usual; it however became more moderate at 5 o'clock, and we were able to continue our route, although the guide seemed much puzzled to keep in the proper direction, there being nothing to serve as marks in this wilderness of snow.

In the afternoon the weather again became worse, and the temperature fell to — 12°, which with a strong head wind made it sufficiently cold. I felt it probably more than the others, as I had to stop often to take bearings, and in consequence was once or twice nearly losing the party altogether. We trudged on manfully until 5 P M., when it cleared up for two or three minutes, and we obtained a distant glimpse of some high islands in the bay for which we were bound, called Ak-koo-lee-gu-wiak by the natives. At half-past 5 we commenced building our snow house. This was far from pleasant work, as the wind was piercingly cold, and the fine particles of snow drift penetrated our clothes everywhere; we, however, enjoyed ourselves the more when we got under shelter and took our supper of the staple commodities, pemmican and water. Latitude 68° 51′ N., longitude 89° 16′ W.

15th.—It blew a complete storm all night, but we were as snug and comfortable, in our snow hive, as if we had been lodged in the best house in England. At 5.30 the wind moderated to a gale, but the drift was still so thick that it was impossible to see any distance before us, particularly when looking to windward, and that unfortunately was the direction in which we had to go. The temperature was 21° below zero,—a temperature which, as all Arctic travellers know, feels much colder, when there is a breeze of wind, than one of —60° or —70° when the weather is calm. But there was. the prospect of both food and fuel before us, for seals were said to abound in the bay and heather on the islands of Akkooleeguwiak. Such temptations were not to be resisted; so we muffled ourselves well up and set out. It was one of the worst days I had ever travelled in, and I could

not take the bearings of our route more than once
or twice.

To make matters worse, one of our dogs, a fine
lively little creature, that was a great favourite
with us all, became unable to walk unharnessed,
and the men having enough to do with the sledges,
I dragged, carried, and coaxed it on for a few
miles ; but finding that some parts of my face were
freezing, and that my companions were so far
ahead as to be out of sight, I was reluctantly compelled to leave the poor animal to its fate.

After a most devious course of nearly twelve miles,
we came to the shores of the bay.   The banks were
of mud and shingle, about sixty or seventy feet high,
and so steep that it was some time before we could
find a place by which to get down to the ice.   We
directed our steps among much rough ice towards
the highest of the group of islands named Coga-ur-
ga-wiak, apparently six miles distant, and encamped
near its western end in a little well-sheltered bay.
All the party, even the Esquimaux, had got severely
frost-bitten in the face, but as it was not much more
than skin deep, this gave us little concern.   When
our house was nearly built, a search was commenced
among the snow for heather, and we were so fortunate as to procure enough in an hour and a-half to
cook us some pemmican and flour, in the form of a
kind of soup or pottage.

We were all very glad to get into our blankets as

soon as possible. The weather became somewhat finer in the evening, but it drifted as much as ever. The thermometer was —16°. Our latitude was 68° 53′ 44″ N., longitude 89° 55′ 30″ west. Notwithstanding that I carried my watch next my skin the cold stopped it, and I could not tell exactly the time of our arrival at the island, but I believed it was near 2 P.M.

On the 16th, a gale of wind from N.W. with thick drift, and the thermometer at —20°, would have prevented our travelling had I intended it; but as I purposed leaving some of the men and all the dogs here to recruit, I wished to find out the Esquimaux (who we knew were in the neighbourhood, as the recent foot tracks of two had been seen on the shore the day before), and obtain from them some seals' flesh and blubber for our use. Flett, Ivitchuk, and the interpreter were sent on this mission, but they returned in the evening unsuccessful. The drift was so thick in the bay that they could not see to any distance. In the meantime Corrigal and Adamson had been collecting fuel, and I being under the lee of the island obtained observations for latitude and variation of the compass, the former being 68° 53′ 44″ north as above, the latter 87° 40′ west.

I prepared for an early start the next morning in company with Flett and Corrigal, for the purpose, if possible, of reaching Sir John Ross's most southerly discoveries, which could not now be distant more than two days' journey.

The party that were to be left behind had orders to kill seals, (for which purpose Ivitchuk was furnished with a spear,) to trade provisions from the Esquimaux if they saw any, and, above all, to use as little of our present stock as possible. All that we could afford to take with us was four days' scanty allowance. I had for the last week carried my instruments, books, &c., in all about thirty-five pounds weight; and I now intended to do the same.

The morning of the 17th was stormy and cold (—22°), and we did not start until near 6 o'clock; when we had got well clear of the S.W. end of the island, we found the ice smooth, and the snow on it hard-packed. As the men had but a light load we travelled fast, our course being nearly N.W. towards the farthest visible land in that direction. A brisk walk of seventeen miles brought us, an hour before noon, to the shore near a high point formed of dark gray granite, which I named Cape Berens, after one of the Directors of the Company. It is situated in latitude 69° 4' 12" N. by observation, and longitude 90° 35' 48" W. by account. The shore, which was steep and rocky, ran nearly in a straight line, and in the same direction that we had been already travelling. At 3 P.M. we came to two narrow points in a small bay, between which we built our snow-house. To these points I gave the name of "the Twins." Their latitude is 69° 13' 14" N., longitude 90° 55' 30" W.

There being one or two hills at a short distance

from us, I ascended one of them to look for fuel, and to gain a view of our future route. I obtained neither of these objects, but fell in with some lead ore, specimens of which were brought away.

On arriving at the snow-hut I found it nearly completed, but so small that there was little prospect of a comfortable night's rest. Having but a very small quantity of alcohol for fuel, our supper was a cold one. Thermometer in the evening 19° below zero. Flett (one of Dease and Simpson's best men) showed symptoms of fatigue, at which I was much surprised, as, from what I had heard of him, I fancied he would have tired out any of the party.

18th.—My anticipations of passing an uncomfortable night were fully realized. It might be thought that, as our whole bedding consisted of one blanket, and a hairy deer-skin to put between us and the snow, there was reason enough for my not sleeping soundly; but this was not the case, as I often passed nights both before and after this with as little covering, but never found myself cold. We started at 3 A.M. The morning was fine but hazy, with a light air of wind from N.W. Thermometer —3°. The walking was still fair; and I may here remark, that wherever the land had an eastern exposure the ice was smooth, there being little or none of the former year forced up along the shore; whenever the coast was exposed to the west, the contrary was the case.

Our course was nearly that of the previous day,

but a little more to the westward. After walking twelve miles we came to what proved to be the head of a deep inlet, the western shore of which we had been tracing, and which I named after John Halkett, Esq., one of the Directors of the Hudson's Bay Company, whose son (Lieut. P. A. Halkett, R.N.,) is the ingenious inventor of the portable air-boat, which ought to be the travelling companion of every explorer. Two reindeer were seen here.

As there could be no doubt that, if my longitude was correct, I must now be near the Lord Mayor's Bay of Sir John Ross, I decided on striking across land, as nearly north as possible, instead of following the coast. The men having had a short time to rest, we commenced a tiresome march over land, the snow being in some places both deep and soft. We crossed three small lakes, and at noon, when near the middle of another about four miles long, an excellent meridian observation of the sun gave latitude 69° 26′ 1″ N. When we had walked three miles more we came to another small lake; and here, as there was yet no appearance of the sea, I ordered my men to prepare our lodgings, whilst I went on alone to endeavour to discover the coast.

A walk of twenty minutes brought me to an inlet not more than a quarter of a mile wide. This I traced to the westward for upwards of a league, when my course was again obstructed by land. There were some high rocks near at hand which I ascended, and from the summit I thought I could distinguish rough ice in the desired direction. With renewed hopes I slid down a declivity, plunging among snow, scrambling over rocks, and through rough ice until I gained more level ground. I then directed my steps to some rising ground which I found to be close to the seashore. From the spot on which I now stood, as far as the eye could reach to the north-westward, lay a large extent of ice-covered sea, studded with innumerable islands. Lord Mayor's Bay was before me, and the islands were those named by Sir John Ross the Sons of the Clergy of the Church of Scotland.

The isthmus which connects the land to the north with the continent is only one mile broad, and even in this short space there are three small ponds. From the great number of stone marks set up (the only ones that I saw on this part of the coast), I am led to infer that this is a deer-pass in the autumn, and consequently a favourite resort of the natives. Its latitude is 69° 31′ N., longitude by account 91° 29′ 30″ W. This latter differs only a mile or two from that of the same place as laid down by Sir James C. Ross, with whose name I distinguished the isthmus, calling the land to the northward Sir John Ross's Peninsula. After going down to the ice in Hardy Bay, and offering with a humble and grateful heart thanks to Him who had thus brought our journey so far to a successful termination, I began to retrace my steps towards my companions.

At a late hour I reached our snow hut, an excellent roomy one, in which we could lie in any position ; no trifling comfort after a walk of more than forty miles over a rough road.

It was 7 o'clock the following morning before we started. The weather was pleasant, and the thermometer 12° below zero. Having taken possession of our discoveries with the usual formalities, we traced the inlet eastward, the shores of which were steep and rugged, in some places precipitous. When we had walked four miles the land on our left turned up to the northward, leaving an opening in that direction more than two miles wide, bounded on the south-east by one or more islands. This inlet I named after that celebrated navigator and discoverer Sir John Franklin, whose protracted absence in the Arctic Sea is at present exciting so much interest and anxiety throughout England. The most distant visible point was called Cape Thomas after a relative. The land on our right still trended to the east for two miles, and then turned to the south. After walking seven miles in this last direction, and passing two small bays and as many points, we stopped for the night. Here we were fairly puzzled about the proper route, there being so many inlets and small bays that it was impossible to tell which was the one we ought to follow. The day had become very warm, the thermometer rising as high as + 26° in the sun, and as we were now travelling south, we found the reflection from the snow much more painful to the eyes than when proceeding north. The latitude of our snow house was 69° 22′ N., longitude 91° 3′ W., both by account. The thermometer —19° in the evening; cold water and pemmican for supper, and kettles of snow for bedfellows.

The morning of the 20th was cold, but calm; thermometer —24°. We commenced our day's march at 2 h. 30 m. A.M., and in twenty minutes arrived at the head of the inlet where I hoped to find a passage. Seeing that it would be madness to trace all the indentations of this most irregular coast, (for had a couple of days' stormy weather ensued we should all have run the risk of starving,) I struck over land towards our snow hut of the 17th.

This was the most fatiguing and at the same time the most ludicrous march we had experienced. As our route lay across several ranges of hills, we had no sooner climbed up one side than we had to slide down the other. To descend was not always an easy matter, as there were often large stones in the way, past which we required to steer with great care, or if a collision was unavoidable, to manage so as not to injure ourselves. Corrigal appeared to be an old hand at this sort of work, and I had had some practice, but poor Flett, who had begun to suffer much from inflammation of the eyes, got many queer falls, and was once or twice placed in such situations with his head down hill, his heels up, and the strap of his bundle round his neck, that it would have been impossible for him to get up by his own unaided exertions.

After crossing a number of small lakes, we arrived at the steep shores of Halkett Inlet about 11 o'clock, having been eight hours in walking as many miles. We crossed the inlet, and as it had now begun to blow a fresh breeze we stopped at a small bay, well sheltered, to take some rest, and obtain a meridian observation of the sun. The latitude was 69° 16′ 44″ N., variation of the compass 76° 45′ W. We were so fortunate as to find here some heather by scraping away the snow, and we enjoyed the luxury of a cup of chocolate, which refreshed us very much.

We now resumed our march, and the walking being good and the day fine we made rapid progress, although somewhat detained by the lameness and blindness of Flett, who stumbled at every inequality of the ground, and received some severe falls. After advancing two miles we came opposite to a clear opening to the north-eastward, in which nothing but rough ice could be seen. This was evidently the termination of the continent in this direction. At 4 P.M. we arrived at our snow hut in the small bay between the Twins. It was not my intention to remain here all night, but the lameness of our companion prevented us from continuing our journey. Whilst I went to search for fuel, Corrigal enlarged our snow house. I found a little fuel, with which we contrived to thaw as much snow as gave each of us nearly half-a-pint of water. The remainder of our provisions, amounting to a few ounces of pemmican each, was fairly divided, and having eaten part of this we betook ourselves to rest.

21st.—Having passed a far from pleasant night, and used the last of our alcohol to procure some water as a diluent for our not very plentiful breakfast, we started at a little before 2 A.M. There was a strong breeze from N.W. with thick drift occasionally, and a temperature of —20°, but the wind being on our backs it was rather an advantage than otherwise. We directed our course straight for the island on which we had left the rest of the party, and which could be seen at intervals when the snow drift cleared away.

Flett being still very lame, I desired Corrigal to remain in company with him, whilst I went on alone to order some provisions to be prepared by the time they came to the snow house. The ice being smooth, and the snow on its surface hard, I made rapid progress until within about five miles of our temporary home. Here I observed some strange looking figures on the ice, which the thickness of the weather prevented me from seeing distinctly. On a nearer approach I found that what had puzzled me was a number of Esquimaux spears, lances, &c. stuck on a heap of snow; and immediately afterwards four Esquimaux came from behind a mound of ice, holding up their hands to show that they were unarmed. The natives of this part of the coast bear a very bad character, and are much feared by their countrymen of Repulse Bay. I therefore was not quite sure what sort of reception I might meet with, as my men were not in sight and I was quite unarmed. But to anticipate evil is often the most likely way to cause it, so I went directly up, and saluted them with their usual term for peace (teyma), shaking hands with all after the fashion of our own country. They all shouted out Manig Tomig, which are the words mentioned by Sir John Ross as the form of salutation employed by the natives of Boothia Felix. A very animated conversation soon ensued, in which I bore but a very small share; but as I appeared to be a good listener, and put in a negative or affirmative every now and then when there appeared to be a necessity for saying something, we got on very well together.

We were soon joined by an old woman who took upon herself the office of mistress of the ceremonies, and commenced with great volubility to give me the names of the men, which were as follows :—A-li-ne-a-yuk, Kag-vik, Tag-na-koo and Nu-li-a-yuk ; the first being old, the second middle aged, and the two last young men of about twenty-five. They were all married, and were much more forward in their manners and dirty in their persons and dress, than our friends of Repulse Bay. They were very anxious for me to enter their huts, but this I thought it prudent to decline, and after much persuasion and promises of knives, needles, beads, &c. I prevailed on them to follow me to our snow house.

A little more than an hour brought me to our encampment, where I found Adamson quite well but

all alone, Ivitchuk and the boy being out looking
for seals. They had not met with any Esquimaux,
and no animals of any kind had been killed,
Ivitchuk standing so much in awe of his countrymen that he was afraid to stay out seal-hunting
during the night, which is the only time that these
animals are to be caught at that season of the year.
I found that much more of our stock of provisions
had been used than there was any occasion for—in
fact, the appearance of the men shewed that they
had been on full allowance.

About an hour after my arrival, Corrigal and
Flett made their appearance, accompanied by the
four Esquimaux that I had seen and a boy. A few
trifling presents were made them, and they promised
to return on the following day with oil, blubber, &c.
to barter with us. It blew a gale all the evening,
with the thermometer 21° below zero.

The morning of the 22d was fine with a temperature of —20°, but during the day it blew hard with
drift. Our party kept in bed rather longer than usual,
and we were visited by the Esquimaux before we
had got up. They brought a quantity of seal's flesh,
blood, and blubber, which I was about to purchase
from them when the thermometer was reported as
missing. I immediately shut the box containing
the valuables, and intimated that they should receive
nothing unless the thermometer was given up. After
about ten minutes' delay one of the women brought
in the lost article, saying, that the dogs had pulled

it down and carried it off, — a very probable story
certainly ; but having obtained what I wanted I
cared little who might be the thief.

A brisk traffic was soon commenced for oil, seals,
blubber, flesh and blood, for which knives, files,
beads, needles, &c. were given. We also obtained
half a dozen dried salmon and a small piece of
dried musk-ox flesh, both very old and mouldy.
These Esquimaux were found to be much more
difficult to deal with than our friends of Repulse
Bay, being very forward and much addicted to
stealing. They had undoubtedly had commu-
nication with the natives of Boothia Felix, as there
were many of their weapons, and parts of their
sledges formed of oak. I also observed some small
pieces of mahogany among them. One of the
strangers proved to be an uncle of Ivitchuk.

It continued to blow hard in the evening with a
temperature of —15°. Preparations were made for
examining the shores of the bay in which, by Esquimaux report, we now were.

23d. This was another stormy and cold day
until the afternoon, when it became fair. We were
again visited by our neighbours, who brought us a
further and very acceptable supply of seals' flesh and
blood, and also two fine dogs to complete our teams,
one or two of those we had being still very weak.

When about to make a tour round the bay,
I learnt from one of the natives that a complete
view of its shores could be obtained from the sum-

mit of the island on which we were. I found also
that a chart which he made of the bay agreed very
closely with one drawn by the natives of Repulse
Bay, who had visited the place. The evening being
beautifully clear, I took with me the Esquimaux,
one of the men, and the interpreter to the highest
point of the island, from which I obtained a distinct
view of the whole bay, except a small portion immediately under the sun. The shores were high and
regular in their outline, and being, in most places,
to a certain extent denuded of snow, they were much
more clearly seen than could have been expected.
The bay appeared to extend 16 or 18 miles slightly
to the east of south, and was about 11 miles wide
near its head. Its surface was studded with a number of dark-coloured rocky islands. The highest of
these was the one on which we were staying, and
was found by measurement to be 730 feet above the
level of the sea. It was called Helen Island, whilst
the group to which it belonged was named after
Benjamin Harrison, Esq. one of the Directors of the
Hudson's Bay Company. The Esquimaux pointed
out the direction in which two rivers near the head
of the bay lay. These rivers, of which I took the
bearings by compass, were said to be of no great
size, and frozen to the bottom in winter. The bay
was honoured with the name of Sir John H. Pelly,
Bart., Governor of the Company.

The morning of the 24th was as beautiful as could
be desired, with the thermometer at —15°. There

was a gentle air from the east, and the horizon being very clear, I again obtained a fine view of the bay.

Having abundance of blubber for dogs' meat and fuel, and as much seals' flesh and blood for ourselves as at half allowance would serve us for six or seven days, I determined to trace the shores of the land across which we had travelled on our outward journey.

For this purpose, both men and dogs being now much recruited, we started at 8 h. 30 m. A.M. and took a N. E. by E. course towards the eastern shore of the bay, which, having a western exposure, was much encumbered with rough ice. We had some trouble in getting over this, but found it more smooth along the shore, which trended due north. Finding that our sledges were too heavily laden, we left on the ice a quantity of our oil and blubber. Here we made a mistake in retaining the fresh fat of the seal, instead of that which had become somewhat rancid, as we found that, although the dogs ate the latter with avidity, they would scarcely taste the former. This Ivitchuk well knew, but he was too stupid to tell me of it at the time. One of our dogs that had done his work well since leaving Repulse Bay, had become so weak that he could scarcely walk. We endeavoured to coax him on, but unsuccessfully; it was therefore thought advisable to leave him where we had lightened our load, as he would have provisions for at least a fortnight, if not assisted by other animals, and before that time he would very likely be found by the Esquimaux. A meridian observation gave latitude 68° 56′ 46″ N., variation 78° 56′ W.

As the sun had acquired too much power for travelling comfortably during the day-time, I stopped early so as to be able to continue our journey about midnight. Our snow hut was built near a small creek, in latitude 68° 58′ N., longitude 89° 42′ W. The coast had become low and flat, with a few fragments of lime-stone and granite boulders showing themselves occasionally above the snow. The thermometer exposed to the sun's rays rose to + 37°. A little snow fell in the evening.

On the morning of the 25th there was some more snow with a temperature of — 7°. We did not commence our march until some hours later than I had expected. The direction of the land continued nearly north for eight miles; it then turned off to the north-east, and continued so until we stopped at noon, in latitude by observation 69° 14′ 37″ N. longitude by account 89° 18′ 18″ W. The tracks of a large Polar bear and of some lemmings were noticed this day.

26th.—The morning was dark and cloudy when we started at 20 minutes after one. When just about to set out, we were joined by the poor dog we had left behind. He had grown into much better condition, although he was still unable to haul. I may here add that he afterwards quite recovered, and was the only one of our stock that I took to England with me.

Our course for seven miles was east, and then turned off S. E. by S. forming a cape, which was named Chapman, after one of the Directors of the Hudson's Bay Company.

We continued walking on, in nearly a straight line, for 11 miles, when our dogs became tired, and we encamped an hour before noon, in latitude by observation 69° 5′ 35″ N., variation 81° 50′ W., longitude by account 88° 43′ W. At 11 P.M. we recommenced our march, the weather being beautiful, and the temperature —8°.

27th.—The coast trended in exactly the same direction as that we had passed during the latter part of the preceding day's journey; the walking was in general good, and our dogs were every day recovering their strength. A single rock grouse *(tetrao rupestris)* was seen, but so shy that we could not get a shot at it. Many traces of foxes, and the recent foot-marks of a large white bear, were also seen. We kept a sharp out-look for the latter, with the hopes of getting a few steaks out of him, but he did not show himself. There was a high wall of broken ice all along the shore here, which may be readily accounted for by the direction of the coast, which, by contracting the bay, is exposed to the pressure of the ice coming from the northward. Fortunate it was for us that we had got some oil and seals' blubber, for there was not a bit of anything in the shape of fuel to be seen along this barren shore. The weather having become too warm, about 11

A.M., we stopped in latitude, by observation, 68° 51′ N., longitude by account 88° 6′ W.

The morning of the 28th was particularly fine, with a temperature of 15° below zero. For eight miles our course was the same as that of the day before, but the land now turned gradually to the southward, and finally to about a south-by-west direction. At noon the sun had become so warm, that we were compelled to encamp for the day. At three miles from where we had stopped, we passed a small bay, about 1½ mile wide, the only indentation of the coast we had seen since leaving Pelly Bay. Our latitude by meridian observation was 68° 32 40″ N., variation of the compass 70° 55′ W., and our longitude by account 88° 2′ W.

29th.—We resumed our march at a little after 11 P.M. on the 28th. The weather was calm, but cloudy, with the temperature — 3°. The line of coast now ran nearly south, and after a walk of five miles we came to a narrow point, extending two miles to the eastward. We then crossed a bay about 1½ mile wide, and arrived at another point of nearly the same dimensions, both formed of mud and shingle. These I named respectively after James and Robert Clouston, two intimate friends.

Four miles further brought us opposite to a small low island, half a mile from the shore, and at a short distance beyond this we came to a small bay upwards of a mile wide. A little before noon we stopped to build our snow hut. The day was now

K

warm, the thermometer having risen as high as + 55° in the sun, and + 18° in the shade. One of our best dogs got lamed by putting his foot into a crack in the ice. We saw the smoke of open water at no great distance, and heard the ice making a loud noise as it was driven along with the tide. There were numerous traces of foxes, and the tracks of a band of deer, with a wolverine in pursuit, were noticed. The latitude of our position was 68° 15′ N., variation 75° 52′ W., and longitude by account 88° 5′ 36″ W.

30th.—We started at half-past nine the previous night, with clear weather and a fresh breeze from west, which, with a temperature of — 8°, made our already frost-bitten faces smart severely. After a few miles' walk, we rounded a low spit of land, which had been hid from our view by the rough ice on our outward journey, and which I now named Point Anderson. Between this point and Cape Barclay, of which we now got sight, there is a narrow bay running up to the northward two or three miles.

We had a great quantity of rough ice to scramble over, which, however fatiguing, afforded some amusement, as the ridiculous positions in which we were sometimes placed gave abundant food for mirth to those who were disposed to look at every thing in the most favourable light.

About midnight the weather became very stormy, so much so indeed that we had great difficulty in

keeping the proper course, which was now to the
north west, for the purpose of picking up the pemmican, &c. which we had deposited on the shore of
Keith Bay on the 12th. On reaching the west side
of the bay at 3 A.M. I found that we were not
more than a hundred yards from where our " cache"
was placed, which we found quite safe. Ivitchuk
and the boy having lagged behind, we removed a
quantity of snow, and took possession of our old
snow hut to wait for them. After staying for an
hour we resumed our journey, thinking that our
companions might have taken a shorter route across
the bay ; and this we found to be the case. It had
been cold and stormy during the greater part of
the night; but at 8 h. 30 m. A.M., when we encamped opposite Cape Beaufort, the weather had
become beautiful.

The whole of the coast which we had traced
during the last seven days, as far as Cape Barclay,
was low and flat, with neither rock nor hill to
interrupt the sameness of the landscape. It was
named Simpson's Peninsula after Sir George Simpson, the able and enterprising Governor of the
Hudson's Bay Company's territories, who projected
and planned the expedition, and to whose zeal in the
cause of discovery Arctic travellers have been so
often and so much indebted.

During the remainder of our journey homewards,
having followed as nearly as possible our outward
route, we met with little of any interest. We reached

our encampment of the 9th of April on the 1st of May, and found our " cache " of provisions quite safe. We had now an abundant stock of food, nor were we sorry to exchange the seals' flesh and blood, on which we had been subsisting for eight days past, for pemmican and flour. It is true that during that time we had supped on a few dried salmon, which were so old and mouldy that the water in which they were boiled became quite green. Such, however, is the advantage of hard work and short commons, that we enjoyed that change of food as much as if it had been one of the greatest delicacies. Both the salmon, and the water in which they were cooked, were used to the last morsel and drop, although I firmly believe that a moderately well fed dog would not have tasted either.

We now saw numerous tracks of rein-deer, all proceeding in a N.E. direction towards Melville Peninsula. Early on the morning of the 3rd of May we arrived at the small lake near Point Hargrave, on which we had encamped on the 7th of April; much of the snow had disappeared from the ground in the neighbourhood, and the marmots had already cleared out the entrances to their burrows, and recommenced their life of activity for the summer season. Not an hour now passed without our seeing deer; but they were extremely shy, and the only benefit we received from them was the life and spirit their presence infused into our dogs.

The night of the 4th was very unpleasant, there

being much snow and drift, which prevented us from seeing the ridges of snow which occurred frequently on our path, and which being very hard and slippery, caused us many falls. At half-past 1 on the morning of the 5th we reached some old Esquimaux dwellings on the border of Christie Lake, about fifteen miles from Fort Hope, in one of which we took up our temporary abode. At 2 P.M. on the same day we were again on the march, and arrived at our home at 8 h. 30 m. P.M. all well, but so black and scarred on the face from the combined effects of oil, smoke, and frost bites, that our friends would not believe but that some serious accident from the explosion of gunpowder had happened to us. Thus successfully terminated a journey little short of 600 English miles, the longest, I believe, ever made on foot along the Arctic coast.

During our absence every thing had gone on prosperously at winter quarters. The people had been all in good health, and the wound in Oulig-buck's arm had healed up, but the limb had not yet acquired much strength. When I set out on the 5th of April there was but a very small quantity of venison in store, so that I was afraid that Folster (the man left in charge) would be forced to use pemmican, which substantial article I wished to save as much as possible for future contingencies. Fortunately the Esquimaux brought a little venison to barter, which, with an occasional deer killed by the hunters, kept the party in food; although the store at one time was so empty, that they were compelled to have a dinner of tongues, which (except in case of necessity) were to be kept for journeys. As the weather in the latter part of April became stormy, and the deer numerous, the hunters were more successful, and there was no further scarcity. Ouligbuck had, notwithstanding the wound in his arm, killed four deer, and sixteen more had been shot by Nibitabo and some others of the party; so that the meat store was well stocked when I arrived; and well that it was so, for we were as ravenous as wolves, and I believe ate more than would have been good for us had our food been anything but venison, which is so digestible that a person may eat almost any quantity without feeling any bad effects from it.

May commenced with a beautiful day, the thermometer being above zero, and continuing so throughout. This was the only day for many months past that the negative scale of the thermometer had not been registered. On the 3rd snowbirds were seen, and marmots had some time before emerged from their winter quarters.

The Esquimaux, with the exception of one or two families, had built their snow huts within a quarter of a mile of our house, where they had been living for more than a week. They had almost all behaved well, and were commended accordingly. They had not yet commenced seal hunting, but were to do so as soon as the seals came up on the ice; in the meantime they were catching deer in snow traps made by digging holes in the snow, and covering them with thin slabs of the same material. Wolves are often taken in a similar manner ; but for them the hole requires to be not less than eight or nine feet deep, and after it is covered with a thin plate of hard snow (on the centre of which a bait is laid), a wall is built round it, over which it is necessary for the wolf to leap, before he can reach the bait. He does so, and falls to the bottom of the pit, which is too .narrow to give him room to make a spring to the top.

I may now say a few words about our travelling companion Ivitchuk, who had behaved well throughout the journey. We found him always willing and obedient, and generally lively and cheerful except when very tired, which was frequently the case, as he had not been accustomed to travel so many days consecutively. He accommodated himself easily to our manners and customs in every respect, living as we did, though he would swallow a piece of seal's blubber now and then as a delicacy. What surprised me most was, that he was by no means a very great eater, being often satisfied with as little as any of the party. Tea and chocolate were favorite beverages with him, and he had learned to smoke his pipe as regularly as if he had been accustomed to it all his life. He picked up a few words of English, which he made use of whenever he thought they were applicable, and was very anxious to be taught to read and write. As he, like the rest of the party, was much thinner than when he commenced the journey, he had made up his mind to do nothing during the remainder of the spring but eat, drink, and sleep, a determination to which I believe he most strictly adhered. It was with no small pride that he received a gun and some ammunition, as a reward for his services; and a few presents to his wife, one of the best looking of the fair sex of Repulse Bay, made the pair quite happy, although it was said that the lady had not behaved very well to her liege lord during his absence, having taken unto herself another husband named Ou-plik; but probably the good man knew nothing, or cared little, about it.

Part of the men were now every day occupied in scraping among the snow for moss and heather, of which a sufficient quantity was procured to keep the kettle boiling.

On Sunday the 9th divine service was read, and thanks offered to the Almighty for having guided us in safety threugh the late journey. Many Esquimaux were present, who conducted themselves with propriety.

CHAPTER VII.

Preparations for exploring the coast of Melville Peninsula—Outfit —Leave Fort Hope— Pass over numerous lakes —Guide at fault —Dease Peninsula—Arrive at the sea—Fatigue party sent back to Fort Hope—Barrier of ice—Lefroy Bay—Large island named after the Prince of Wales—Detained by stormy weather—Short allowance—Cape Lady Simpson—Selkirk Bay—Snow knee-deep—Capes Finlayson and Sibbald—Deer shot—A cooking scene—Favourite native relish—Again stopped by stormy weather—Cape M'Loughlin—Two men left to hunt and fish—Cape Richardson—Chain of islands—Garry Bay — Prince Albert range of hills—Cape Arrowsmith — Coast much indented— Baker Bay—Provisions fail—Proceed with one man—Cape Crozier—Parry Bay—Cape Ellice, the farthest point seen—Take possession—Commence our return—No provisions procured by the men left behind—Short commons—Flock of cranes—Snow-blindness—Arrive at Repulse Bay.

ON the 12th of May preparations were commenced for a journey along the west side of Melville Penin-sula. In expectation of falling in with much rough ice, I determined on taking dogs only for the first three days of the journey. The party was to consist of Corrigal (our snow-house builder), Folster, Matheson, and Mineau, with Ouligbuck as deer-hunter and interpreter. A fatigue party of two men, and an Esquimaux with a sledge and good team of dogs, were to accompany us for three days, which I supposed would be the time required to reach the coast.

Our provisions for the journey were two bags of pemmican, each 90 lbs., 70 reindeer tongues weighing nearly 30 lbs., 36 lbs. flour, and a little tea, chocolate, and sugar. We took also a gallon and a half of alcohol and a small quantity of oil.

Leaving George Flett in charge at Fort Hope, we started at 10 P.M. on the 13th of May, and directed our course towards a chain of lakes in nearly a due north direction. Although the snow was soft, and we had some rather steep rising grounds to pass over, we made good progress, and after crossing six small lakes we came to some high table-land, on which the snow was very deep, and in which the sledge sank very much. A walk of four miles brought us to another lake of considerable size. A little after 6 A.M. on the 14th, we found some snow huts that had been inhabited during part of the winter by the Esquimaux Ecouchi, and soon had one of them cleared out for the accommodation of the party.

Although we had not travelled much more than twenty miles, Ouligbuck was so fatigued that I determined to send him back with those who were to return to Repulse Bay. We saw no game and only very few tracks of deer. The weather was so cloudy that no meridian observation of the sun could be obtained. Our latitude was 66° 52′ N., and longitude 86° 46′ W., both by account.

We resumed our march at 9 P.M. on the 14th, the night being calm, with a little snow falling. A brisk walk of two miles to the N.W. brought us to the end of the lake, when we followed the bed of a small stream to the northward for five miles. Two narrow lakes were next traversed, when our guide, who appeared to know little about the proper route, led us to the N.W.; and after crossing five lakelets, and as many short portages, at half-past 6 A.M. we came to a body of water about the size of that near which we had encamped the day before. Here we stopped for the day. The ice on this lake was six feet thick, and gave the men much trouble to cut through it. There was very little fuel to be found; we were therefore obliged to burn part of the small quantity of oil we had taken with us. By a meridian observation our latitude was 67° 5′ 3″ N., variation of the compass 53° 30′ W., and longitude by account 87° 8′ 54″ W. The west side of the creek, and also of the lakes which we passed over this day, was steep and rocky, although not high; the east sides were more sloping.

It was near 10 o'clock at night when we commenced our journey. After an hour's walk we came to the north end of the lake, but our young Esquimaux never having been here before (which was rather surprising, as his usual winter home was not more than ten miles distant), was quite at a loss what direction to take. It would have been quite easy for me to have made a straight course by compass, but by doing so we were very likely to get among ground so uneven, as to be impassable to the dogs and sledge. We now turned to the east of north, and after crossing a number of small lakes, arrived at the sea (which here formed a deep inlet) at a few minutes before midnight. Proceeding down the inlet, which for a couple of leagues was not more than half a mile wide, with steep rocky shores (in some places precipitous), we came to rough ice, and found that there were apparently two openings leading to the northward. I chose the one to the left, but we had not gone more than a mile-and-a-half, when we found that we were in an arm of the inlet, and that the land to the north of us, which I had supposed to be an island, was joined to the mainland by an isthmus not more than 50 yards wide. This peninsula I named after P. W. Dease, Esq., the able leader, in conjunction with T. Simpson, of the expeditions which explored so large a portion of the Arctic shores in 1837, 1838, and 1839.

Retracing our steps, we now followed the opening to the right, in which there were great quantities of rough ice, over which we advanced but slowly. The inlet (to which I had given the name of Cameron, after a friend), soon became broader and the ice less rough. At 7 A.M. on the 16th we arrived at the Cape, which last autumn had been named after the late Thomas Simpson, whose agreeable duty it would have been, had he survived, to accomplish the survey which I was now endeavouring to bring to a successful termination. The shores here were very barren, there being little or no vegetation to be seen, except small patches in the crevices of the rocks. In a small lake near our encampment, from which we obtained water, the ice was found to be five feet thick. A sufficient quantity of fuel was gathered to boil our kettle, and two hares were shot by Corrigal. We here made a " cache " of some pemmican, flour, &c. for our return journey. Our snow hut was built on the south side of the cape, under shelter of rocks, near which there were two small islands.

The sledge was to be sent back to Repulse Bay from this place, and with it Ouligbuck, who from his inability to walk would have been an incumbrance to us. The weather was so cloudy that no observation could be obtained. Our latitude by account was 67° 22′ (which I afterwards found by observation to be nearly three miles too far north), longitude 87° 3′ W. The whole of these three days' journeys had been measured with a well stretched line, but this we could not expect to carry on further, as each person would have enough to do with his load.

Bidding adieu to our companions who were to return to Fort Hope, we commenced our journey at half-past 8 P. M., each of my men being laden

142

with about 70 lbs., whilst I carried my instruments, books, and some other articles, weighing altogether 40 lbs. This was but a light burden for me, but as I had to examine different objects on the route, and also to lead the way, I found it quite enough.

As soon as we had fairly rounded Cape T. Simpson, the coast turned to the eastward, and became indented with narrow but deep inlets, all of which were packed full of rough ice. Walking became most difficult. At one moment we sank nearly waist-deep in snow, at another we were up to our knees in salt water, and then again on a piece of ice so slippery that, with our wet and frozen shoes, it was impossible to keep from falling. Sometimes we had to crawl out of a hole on all fours like some strange-looking quadrupeds; at other times falling backwards we were so hampered by the weight of our loads, that it was impossible to rise without throwing them off, or being assisted by one of our companions. We therefore found it better to follow the shores of the inlets than to cross them, although by doing so we had double the distance to go over. Numerous traces of hares were seen, but we could not afford to lose time in following them.

After passing four inlets having some small islands lying outside of them, we came to a rocky point rather higher than any we had yet met with on this side of the bay. The coast to the eastward of Point Cowie (so named after an old friend) became more level, and instead of granite, was covered with mud, shingle, and fragments of limestone. At half-past 3 A.M., all of us being sufficiently tired with our night's work, we built our snow hut and a small kitchen for cooking. This was our usual practice when we had found, or were likely to find, fuel. In the present instance, we had the good fortune to collect enough to boil a kettle of chocolate, and we consequently enjoyed an excellent supper, if I may so term a meal taken about six in the morning.

The weather had been fine until midnight, when it began to snow and drift, with a strong breeze from the north. Thermometer + 13°. At noon the sky was too much overcast to obtain an observation. Our latitude was 67° 24′ 20″ N., longitude 86° 37′ W. both by account.

When we resumed our journey, at 7 o'clock in the evening of the 17th, there was still a strong breeze from N. N. W. with snow drift, the temperature being + 18°. Our snow hut of the previous day we now found to be on the shore of a large bay, the most distant point of which bore nearly due north. To follow the coast would have cost us a great deal of additional walking; I therefore determined to attempt the traverse of the bay towards the point above referred to. All along the coast there was a belt of rough ice about two miles broad, over which we were forced to pass before reaching some that appeared smoother outside. To cross this barrier occupied us more than two hours, and gave us more

violent exercise than all the remainder of the day's
journey. It was half-past 3 A.M. when we arrived
at the north point of the bay, which was low and
level, with some hills a few hundred feet high,
three or four miles inland. We had passed two
small rocky islands to seaward in the first part of
the night, and there was another close to a bluff
point on the south side of the bay. To this cape
I gave the name of Watt. The bay was called
after Lieut. (now Captain) Lefroy of the Royal
Artillery, whose name is well known to the scientific
world, and of whose kindness in aiding me in my
astronomical studies I retain a most grateful remem-
brance.

We crossed over to Cape W. Mactavish (so named
after William Mactavish, Esquire, chief trader, an
intimate friend, to whom I am much indebted for
assisting me in fitting out the expedition,) and
stopped about three miles beyond it. Here we
built our snow hut, which was found by meridian
observation to be in latitude 67° 42′ 22″ N.; the
variation of the compass 80° 35′ W., and the longitude by account 86° 30′ W. Directly opposite our
encampment, and extending for about seventeen
miles to the northward of it, there was a large island
of table land, with not a single rock *in situ*
to be seen on it. Its southern extremity bore
nearly west (true) from us, and the strait which
separated it from the mainland was not more than a
mile and a half wide. This island was honoured

with the name of His Royal Highness the Prince of Wales, and a smaller one to the south of it was named after Colonel Sabine.

Not a single living animal had been seen all day, but some traces of deer proceeding northward were noticed. We were again fortunate enough to find a little fuel.

Our route on the following night was nearly straight in a N.N.E. direction. The snow was very soft and deep in many places. A few hundred yards from the beach there were steep banks covered with shingle and small boulders of granite, where we usually found the snow less deep, and walking consequently better. After travelling nine miles we came to a considerable creek, about twenty yards wide, in which a deep channel had been worn among the mud and shingle. Near it there were numerous Esquimaux marks set up, and circular tent sites, but all of old date. We continued our march twelve miles further, and at 8 A.M. arrived at another creek somewhat larger than the last, and with higher banks. Here there were also many Esquimaux marks, and I afterwards learned that some parties had resorted hither from Repulse Bay, for the purpose of catching salmon, trout, &c. About an hour before reaching this place we crossed a long and curiously shaped point, which I named Point Hamilton after a near relative. The bay formed by it was called Erlandson.

One of the men, although an able active fellow,

not being used to this sort of exercise, was much
fatigued; and as the weather looked threatening, I
ordered our snow-house to be built—the more
readily as there was fuel to be found. In little
more than a hour and a half we were comfortably
housed, and not long afterwards we had taken our
usual morning meal of pemmican seasoned with a
handful of flour, those forming, when boiled together, a very nourishing and not unpalatable dish.
The temperature all night had been 22° above zero,
being too warm for walking pleasantly; and the
men, having had to exert themselves much, were
glad to get to rest as soon as possible, whilst I
remained up to obtain a meridian observation of
the sun. This gave latitude 67° 58′ 49″ N. Our
longitude by account was 85° 59′ 36″ W. The sun
was too much obscured by clouds to obtain the
variation. We here deposited some pemmican and
a little flour for our return journey.

When we started at 8 h. 30 m. p.m. on the 19th
it blew a gale of wind from S.S.E. with much drift
and snow, the temperature being only 4° below the
freezing point. Fortunately the wind was on our
backs; but the drift was so thick that we were
obliged to follow every turn of the coast, and we
could not see more than twenty yards before us.
When we had travelled six miles we came to a bay
a mile and a half wide, on the north shore of which
there were two strangely shaped rocks of granite,
having the appearance of an old ruin or portion of

a fortress. They were of a square form, each about twenty-five feet high and nearly as much in extent.

Our course now lay due north; but we had not gone more than twelve miles altogether, when the weather became so unpleasant that we were glad to get under shelter, and before we did so, every part of our clothes was penetrated with snow drift. We could obtain no fuel here.

The weather continued so stormy that we were unable to leave our snow-hut until a quarter past 8 P.M. on the 21st. During our detention, finding that our provisions would run short if the walking continued as difficult as it had been, we took only one not overabundant meal during the twenty-four hours. There was still some snow falling, so that I could not take the proper bearings of the land along which we passed. The land, after we had proceeded N.E. for a few miles, turned to the southward of east, forming a bay eight miles wide, which, as it was full of rough ice, we were under the necessity of coasting. This bay was called after the Rt Hon. the Earl of Selkirk, and the cape forming its western boundary was named after the amiable lady of our much respected governor, Sir George Simpson.

The snow was in many places so soft and deep that we sank above the knee at every step, which made our night's march fatiguing in the extreme. On the N.E. side of Selkirk Bay, which is steep and rocky, there was a deep indentation or inlet, into which two small creeks emptied themselves. The land for five miles had a N.W. trending, and again turned up to the eastward of N., forming a high rugged headland, which was named Cape Finlayson, after Duncan Finlayson, Esq., Chief Factor. At three miles from Cape Finlayson we passed Point Barnston, and about four miles beyond this we came to another rocky point, which received the name of Cape Sibbald. The night had now become very disagreeable, with a heavy fall of snow; we persevered notwithstanding, partly crossing and partly coasting a bay heaped with rough ice, and encamped on what I supposed was its northern extremity, but which afterwards turned out to be an island, and to which I gave the name of Glen. The bay we had just passed was called after William G. Smith, Esq., Assistant Secretary to the Hudson's Bay Company.

The snow not being in a good state for building, we were rather longer than usual in getting housed. There was no fuel to be found, so we followed our old plan, and took a kettle or two of snow to bed with us. The temperature was very high for the season, being only 5° below the freezing point.

When we started at a quarter-past 11 on the 22nd, the night was beautifully clear and calm, with the thermometer at 13° below zero. After a three hours' walk we arrived at the north point of a bay, three and a half miles wide, across which we had come. To the bay I gave the name of Fraser, and to the point that of Corcoran, after two intimate friends, chief traders of the Company.

We had not advanced many miles farther, when some deer were noticed at no great distance, feeding on the banks of a stream. Being desirous of procuring some venison if possible, I sent Corrigal (who, with other good qualities, was a very fair shot) after them, and he was fortunate enough to shoot a fine buck. But the buck, though wounded, could still run too fast to be overtaken, and the sportsman was just about to give up the chase when I joined him, and we continued the pursuit together. The deer, having got a considerable way in advance, had lain down, but rose up before we could get within good shooting distance, and was trotting off at a great pace, when, by way of giving him a parting salute, I fired, and very luckily sent a ball through his head, which dropped him. His horns were already about a foot long, and the venison was in fine order for the season of the year.

I immediately returned to the men, who had been busily employed collecting fuel, of which great quantities grew along the borders of the creek, and sent two of them to assist in skinning and cutting up the deer, whilst I and the other men continued to gather heather, as we now anticipated great doings in the kitchen. We placed the greater part of our venison " en cache," but kept the head, blood, leg bones, &c., for present use; and being determined to lose nothing, the stomach was partially cleaned by rubbing it with snow, and then cut up and boiled, which thus made a very pleasant soup, there being enough of the vegetable contents of the paunch to give it a fine green colour, although I must confess that, to my taste, this did not add to the flavour. Having discussed this mess, a second kettle full was prepared, composed of the blood, brains, and some scraps of the meat, which completed our supper.

It is well known that both Esquimaux and Indians are very fond of the contents of the paunch of the rein-deer, particularly in the spring, when the vegetable substances on which the animal feeds are said to be sweeter tasted. I have often seen our hunter, Nibitabo, when he had shot a deer, cut open the stomach, and sup the contents with as much relish as a London alderman would a plate of turtle soup.

The position of our snow-house was in latitude 68° 33′ 26″ N., longitude 85° 20′ 30″ W., both by account.

The weather was so stormy during the 23rd that we could not continue our journey. The thermometer rose as high as +39° in the shade, and the melting of the snow having wet the heather, we were obliged to have recourse to alcohol. Three or four snow buntings and traces of partridges (*tetrao rupestris*) were seen.

On the 24th it still blew a gale of wind from

the east, but there being a partial thaw by the high temperature, there was no drift, and much of the ground was entirely cleared of snow.

In the evening the weather became more moderate, and the thermometer fell to 5° below the freezing point. We started at a few minutes after 10 o'clock, our course being slightly to the east of north. The travelling was still very fatiguing, as we were frequently forced to pass over the rocks, or to walk along the steep drift banks, in order to avoid the rough ice which had been heaped up against the shore. We passed a number of small bays and points, and when we had advanced fifteen miles, came to a high cape, which forms the N.W. promontory of a bay five miles in extent. To the cape I gave the name of M'Loughlin, after the gentleman who has been for many years in charge of the Columbia department, and the bay was called after my much valued friend Nicol Finlayson, Esq., Chief Factor. After passing Cape M'Loughlin we turned to the eastward, toward the head of the bay, and stopped at 7 A.M. near the mouth of a creek, where we took up our quarters for the day.

There was not so much fuel to be found as at our last encampment, but we gathered enough to boil our kettle. Some bands of deer and a few partridges were observed, but we did not waste time in endeavouring to get a shot at them. Since leaving Fort Hope not a day had passed without more or less snow falling, which made the travelling much more difficult than I expected, and our progress consequently so much slower, that, notwithstanding the addition I had made to our stock of provisions, there was some danger of our still running short. I therefore decided on leaving two of the men here to fish and shoot, whilst I went forward with the others.

There was a little snow falling when, along with Corrigal and Matheson, I set out at 10 p.m. on the 25th. The night was mild (6° below freezing) with a light wind from the east. A walk of two miles brought us to a head land, which formed the north side of Finlayson Bay, and which extended seven miles in a W.N.W. direction. To this cape the name of Richardson was given, after the distinguished naturalist, who, having already exposed himself to many dangers and privations in the cause of science, is now about to incur similar hardships in the cause of humanity and friendship, by searching for Sir John Franklin and his gallant party, whose situation, it is too much to be feared, is a critical one.

At the place where we crossed Cape Richardson it was not more than a mile wide, and we found ourselves in a large bay, thickly studded with high and rugged islands. A chain of these islands, which lay outside of us, and to which I gave the name of Pomona, (after the largest island of the Orcadian group,) had effectually served as a barrier to the ice from seaward, and had thus made the walking much smoother than we had hoped to find it. As we advanced there were many tracks of polar bears, and also those of a wolverine, that appeared to follow them very closely, expecting no doubt to appropriate some portion of whatever prey they might catch. A flock of long-tailed ducks passed us, flying to the westward, towards some open water, the vapour exhaled from which appeared in that direction.

As we approached the north side of the bay, which was named after Nicholas Garry, Esq., of the Hudson's Bay Company, there were so many islands that I was much at a loss what direction to take. Under these circumstances we encamped at 6 A.M. on a high island, about two miles in diameter, from which a good view could be obtained. Garry Bay is the most strangely shaped, and the most irregular in its outline, of any we had yet seen. It presented three long, narrow, and high points of land, and had four inlets. The largest and most southerly of these points was called after Lieut. Halkett, R.N., and the most northerly of the inlets received the name of Black Inlet. As no fuel could be obtained here, we were reduced to the necessity of using some more of our alcohol, of which but a small quantity now remained. The men were soon asleep under our single blanket, (for this was all the covering we had for the party,) whilst I remained awake for the purpose of obtaining an observation of the sun at noon. This gave latitude 68° 59′ 15′

N., variation of the compass 88° 26′ W., our longitude by account being 84° 48 W.

All the way between Lefroy and Garry Bays there is a range of hills, from 500 to 800 feet high, about five miles from the coast, which was distinguished by the name of His Royal Highness Prince Albert, consort of our beloved Sovereign.

The weather was beautiful all day, and was equally fine when we commenced our march at half-past nine at night. Our route lay somewhat to the west of north, between two lofty islands, the smaller of which received the name of Gladman, and the larger and most northerly I designated Honeyman, after a brother. Seven miles from our encampment we passed a bluff and precipitous point, the northern extremity of Garry Bay, to which the name of Cape Arrowsmith was given, in honour of John Arrowsmith, Esq., the talented hydrographer to Her Majesty.

The land was now completely serrated with narrow points and inlets, along which we were able to make nearly a straight course, as the force of the ice from the westward had been much broken by ridges of rocks that lay outside of us. To four of these inlets I gave the names of M'Kenzie, Whiffen, Bunn, and Hopkins, after much esteemed friends.

Towards the end of our night's journey the coast turned nearly due north, and when we had advanced seven leagues we encamped on Cape Miles, —so named after Robert Miles, Esq., Chief Factor,—

at 7 A.M. on the 27th. As the morning was exceedingly fine, we thought there was no necessity for building a snow-house, an omission which we regretted in the afternoon, when a heavy fall of snow took place.

By a good meridian observation of the sun, the latitude 69° 19′ 39″ N., and the variation of the compass 92° 20′ west, were obtained, the longitude by account being 85° 4′ W. The latter is evidently erroneous, as I had neither chronometer nor watch that I could place dependence upon, and the compasses were much affected by local attraction.

Our provisions being now nearly all used, I could advance only half a night's journey further to the northward, and return the following morning to our present quarters. Leaving one of the men, I set out with the other at half-past 9 P.M., the snow falling fast; and although we had little or nothing to carry, the travelling was very fatiguing as we crossed Baker Bay—so named in memory of a much valued friend—at the north side of which we arrived after a walk of four miles. It now snowed so thick that we could not see farther than fifty yards round us, and we were consequently obliged to follow the windings of the shore, which, when we had traced it six miles beyond Baker Bay, turned sharp to the eastward; but the weather continuing thick, I could not see how far it preserved this trending. After waiting here nearly an hour, the sky cleared up for a few minutes at 4 A.M., which enabled me to discover that we were on the south shore of a considerable bay, and I could also obtain a distinct view of the coast line for nearly twelve miles beyond it.

To the most distant visible point (latitude 69° 42' N., longitude 85° 8' W.,) I gave the name of Cape Ellice, after Edward Ellice, Esq. M.P., one of the Directors of the Company ; the bay to the northward, and the headland on which we stood, were respectively named after the distinguished navigators Sir Edward Parry and Captain Crozier. Finding it hopeless to attempt reaching the strait of the Fury and Hecla, from which Cape Ellice could not be more than ten miles distant, we took possession of our discoveries with the usual formalities, and retraced our steps, arriving at our encampment of the previous day at half-past 8 A.M. Here we found that Matheson, the man left behind, had built a snow-house after a fashion of his own, the walls being like those of a stone building, and the roof covered in the same way with slabs of snow placed on the opposite walls in a slanting position, so as to rest on one another in the centre. Seven hours had been spent in building this edifice, which was not a very handsome one ; but being sufficiently wide, and, when our legs were doubled up a little, long enough for us all when lying down, we found it pretty comfortable.

During the remaining four hours of our absence, he had been engaged in an attempt to coax a little wet moss into a sufficient blaze to boil some chocolate; but, notwithstanding his most persevering exertions, by the time his fuel was expended, the chocolate was little more than lukewarm, although our cook *pro tempore*, who was of a sanguine temperament, firmly believed that it was just about to reach the boiling point. We finished the process with a little of our remaining stock of alcohol, and enjoyed an excellent though rather scanty supper.

Matheson was one of the best men I ever had under my command. Always ready, willing, and obedient, he did his duty in every respect; and whilst he possessed spirit enough for anything, he had a stock of good humour which never failed him in any situation, however difficult and trying. Were the walking difficult or easy, the loads heavy or light, provisions abundant or reduced to less than half allowance, it was all one to Peter Matheson; he had a joke ready for every occasion.

A few minutes after 10 P.M. on the 28th, we were on the march homeward. The night was very disagreeable, there being a strong breeze of head wind with heavy snow, and a temperature much too mild (only 8° below the freezing point) for walking comfortably. The snow also was very soft, so that, had it not been for the bad state of our victualling department, we would have remained snug in our quarters. But needs must when hunger drives, so we trudged on stoutly, crossing over the land for the purpose of shortening our distance. After a tough walk, during which we met with some tracks of bears that had passed only about an hour before, we encamped on a small island close to Cape Arrowsmith, and nearly three miles to the northward of our snow hut of the 26th. The weather during the day became fine, so fine indeed that our house, not being built of good material, tumbled down about our ears just before we were leaving it.

29th.—When we started at half-past 9 P.M., the night was fine, but in half an hour it began to snow so thick that we could not keep our course in crossing Garry Bay, where the walking was much worse than when we formerly passed. In three hours the weather again cleared up, and I found that we had not deviated much from the right road.

At 7. A.M. we joined Folster and Mineau, whom we found quite well, but like ourselves very thin. The only animals they had killed were two marmots, and no fish had been caught. If we had been twelve hours longer absent, they intended to have boiled a piece of parchment skin for supper, and to have kept the small remaining piece of pemmican for travelling provisions.

I have had considerable practice in walking, and have often accomplished between forty and fifty, and, on one occasion, sixty-five miles in a day on snow shoes, with a day's provisions, blanket, axe, &c. on my back; but our journey hitherto had been the most fatiguing I had ever experienced. The severe exercise, with a limited allowance of food, had much reduced the whole party, yet we were all in excellent health ; and although we lost flesh, we kept up our spirits, and marched merrily on, tightening our belts—mine came in six inches—and feasting our imaginations on full allowance when we arrived at Fort Hope.

On the 30th we continued our course homewards, crossing over the several points that we had formerly coasted. It snowed heavily all night, and the temperature was only two degrees below the freezing point. Eight cranes " winged their circling flight " northward, and half a dozen sandpipers were seen. It was near 4 A.M. on the 31st when we arrived at our snow house of the 23rd, which we found quite as good as when we left it and our cache of venison all safe. Three partridges were shot, which somewhat aided our short commons.

On the following night, after an ineffectual attempt to get to seaward of the rough ice, in which we lost a considerable portion of the skin off our shins, we travelled on the land, making short cuts whenever practicable.

On arriving opposite to Glen Island, we found that it was divided from the shore by a channel not much more than a quarter of a mile wide. There was an inlet a few miles in length to the eastward of it, which was named after the Rev. Mr. Mackar of Kingston, Canada West. This night was the finest we had experienced throughout the journey.

A specimen of trap rock was obtained from

some rising grounds a mile and a half distant from the north shore of Smith's Bay, near the head of which we now for the first time observed a lake of a couple miles in extent. When half a league from Cape Sibbald, we encamped under shelter of some precipitous trap cliffs nearly a hundred feet high. Some more cranes were seen, and numerous traces of deer and partridges. We here procured some fuel, there being patches of ground bare of snow. Our latitude by observation was 68° 19′ 50″ N. Variation of the compass 80° 55′ W. Two of the men were affected with snow blindness—one of them severely.

1st June.—It blew a gale of wind from S. E., with thick snowdrift at 8h. 30m. P.M. when we resumed our journey. At half-past 10 we crossed the largest stream that we had yet met with on Melville Peninsula. It was already partially open, owing to numerous springs, which had formed many small mounds of ice from ten to twelve feet high. After taking a copious draught from the limpid stream, we continued our journey across Point Barnston and Cape Finlayson, until we arrived at Selkirk Bay, when, the weather having become much worse, we stopped at 1h. 30m. A.M. to build our snow hut at a place where there was such an abundant supply of heather, that we had enough to cover our snow-bed with. Two deer were seen, and Corrigal made an ineffectual attempt to get a shot at them. I shot five ptarmigan, and four sandpipers were observed.

During the next night's journey the weather was very snowy, but the wind being more moderate we got on faster. After coasting Selkirk Bay, we cut across Cape Lady Simpson, and at half-past 6 A.M. on the 3rd of June, we reached our encampment of the 19th ultimo in Erlandson Bay, where we found our small " cache " of provisions quite safe. Five more partridges were shot, and some deer seen. The snow being very soft, we remained here all day, and at noon obtained the latitude 67″ 59′ N., and variation 75″ 9′ W. The thermometer in the shade rose as high as +54°, and our old snow-house tumbled down about our ears in the evening, just as we were going to take our supper,—perhaps breakfast would be the more appropriate term, as we had turned day into night.

We started at 8h. 30m. P.M., and notwithstanding the great power of the sun, so much snow had fallen lately that it lay far deeper on the ground than when we had previously passed this way. The walking also was so much more fatiguing, that we were not able to reach our snow-house of the 18th of May, and were in consequence under the necessity of building new lodgings. The night was mild and nearly calm. Two phalaropes (*P. fulicarius*) were seen, and a couple of ptarmigan shot. There was no fuel to be found here, but having picked up a little as we came along, we did not feel the want of it much.

The 4th was a fine night with the thermometer at

M

+23°, when, at 7h. 40m., we resumed our march. Whilst rounding Cape Mactavish we fell in with nine partridges, seven of which were shot, and I endeavoured to get within range of a couple of swans—the first we had seen--but they were too shy. We now crossed Lefroy Bay, the snow on which was very soft, and built our snow-house on the ice at 7h. A.M. about four miles from its south shore. The work during this journey had been so much more severe than was expected, and the men had in consequence used so much more tobacco than they had anticipated, that their stock was now quite exhausted, and they appeared to feel the want as much as if they had been deprived of half their allowance of food,—perhaps more. It was really amusing to see how very particular they were in dividing the small remaining bits which they rummaged from the dust and rubbish in their pockets, and which at any other time they would have thrown away. I happened to have a little snuff with me, a pinch of which, in their necessity, they relished much.

We were on foot again at 20 minutes after 8 on the 5th. The weather had been stormy all day, but became fine an hour after we started. We kept well out from land, expecting to find the ice smoother; and this was the case as far as Point Cowie; but beyond that the rough ice extended quite across the bay ; we therefore struck in for the shore, which after two hours' scrambling we reached, and directed our course over the rocks, —from which the snow had now, in many places, entirely dissappeared,—towards Cape T. Simpson, where we arrived at 5h. A.M. on the 6th, and found our " cache " of provisions, &c., as we had left it. No time was lost in getting the stones cleared away from it, not so much for the purpose of having something to eat, as to find some tobacco that had been left here among other things. A fine hare had been shot, and as soon as three of the party, who had stopped behind to gather fuel, came up, we had a much more abundant and palatable meal than we had enjoyed for many days before. To the large bay, the survey of which we had now completed, the name of Committee Bay was given, in honor of the Committee of the Hudson's Bay Company. This was the finest day we had experienced during this journey, the power of the sun being so great as to raise the thermometer to $+82°$.

By an excellent meridian observation in quicksilver, our latitude was 67° 19′ 14″ N., variation of compass, 64° 27′ W. Wishing to take a straighter, and consequently shorter, route to Repulse Bay than that by which we had gone, we started at 9 P.M. on the 6th, and after a walk of three hours came to the head of a narrow inlet, with high rocky shores, and about seven miles long, to which I gave the name of Munro. Our course overland was nearly due south, and we passed over a number of small lakes, from which the snow had been partially re-

M 2

moved by the joint action of the sun's rays and the wind.

On the following night our course continued the same with a slight inclination to the westward. We had a strong gale of fair wind, which helped us along amazingly ; but as we could easily reach Fort Hope in another night, and as we had abundance of food, we encamped at 3h. 30m. A.M. on the 8th, during the whole of which day, until late in the evening, it blew hard with drifting snow, so that no observations could be made.

Being anxious to arrive at winter quarters early on the following day, we were again on the march at half-past 7 P.M., and the evening having now become fine, we kept up a smart pace for a few hours until we arrived at Christie Lake, where, finding some very fine heather quite dry and free from snow, it was impossible to resist the temptation of having something to eat and drink. Having taken up our quarters in an old snow-hut, the chocolate and pemmican kettles were soon on the fire, and we heartily enjoyed our rather unusual meal. Following the lake and North Pole River, we came to Fort Hope at 8h. 20m. A.M. on the 9th, all in good health and spirits, but very much reduced in flesh, although not quite so black as when we returned from the previous journey.

CHAPTER VIII.

Occurrences at Fort Hope during the absence of the exploring party—Remove from winter quarters to tents—Sun seen at midnight—Build an oven and bake bread—Esquimaux method of catching seals—A concert—Lateness of the summer—A native salmon-wear—Salmon spear—Boulders on the surface of the ice—Visited by a native from the Ooglit Islands—His report of occurrences at Igloolik—Indolence of the natives—Ice breaking up—Halkett's air-boat—A storm—The ice dispersed—Prepare for sea.

DURING my absence from Fort Hope little beyond the usual occurrences of the winter had taken place. The latter part of May was remarkable for the great quantity of snow that fell, with gales of wind and drift, which kept the men almost continually clearing away snow from the roofs of our houses. They were obliged even to go to work during the night, and notwithstanding all the care that was taken, two of the boats' yards were broken, and the masts very nearly shared a like fate, as the post placed under them gave way. For so great a quantity of snow lodging on our roof, the man left in charge was to blame, as shortly after my departure he had the snow thrown up in heaps, which, when the stormy weather and snowdrift came on, caused drift-banks to be raised to an equal height (about 4½ feet) on the tops of our dwellings.

During all this time the thermometer never fell lower than +9°, which was on the 16th of May, and rose as high as +45°, at mid-day on the 29th. The last day of May was very stormy; but on the 1st of June the weather changed for the better, although the thermometer was as low as +12°. On this day the first geese (laughing geese) and some sandpipers were seen, and one of each was shot. As the partridges were migrating northward about thirty had been killed, and there was a good stock of venison in store, the hunters having shot twenty deer. The does were now very large with young, and had become very poor; the bucks were, however, improving in condition.

The Esquimaux had brought in little for trade, a few pairs of boots, which were soon bought up by the men, and a little oil from Akkeeoulik being the principal articles. Some of them were getting short of provisions, not having been able to find a " cache " which they went for. They had all behaved well, not having committed any thefts that could be discovered. We had, however, one most incorrigible thief among our party, Ouligbuck's son, who, during the few days of his father's absence, was twice caught with the old man's bale open, eating sugar; some tobacco was also taken, and the trousers of most of the men were completely cleared of buttons by the same hands. On my return only one family of Esquimaux (Shimakuk's) remained near us. Shimakuk had been waiting for his dogs, which were with the party who had gone in search of meat.

On the 13th divine service was read, and thanks returned to the Almighty for His protection throughout the winter and during the late journey.

There was a strong breeze of N. wind, with frequent showers of snow. House very damp; the clay falling from the inside of the walls.

14th.—The weather was fine and permitted us to get our flour, pemmican, &c., removed from the meat store (which was now dropping much from the roof) to the rocks, where it was well covered up with oilcloths.

The 20th was a most stormy day with occasional showers— wind N.W. There was a considerable stream of water running on the ice of North Pole River, forming large pools on the sea-ice, through which it did not yet find a free exit.

21st.—There was a change in the weather for the better, although it still blew a gale; however, as the day advanced the wind became more moderate, and about noon shifted round to the south.

The water was rising fast in all the creeks, showing that the process of destruction was fast going on among the snow and ice. The latter was still nearly four feet thick on the lakes, but very porous.

The great rise of water in the creeks and small

streams rendered it very unpleasant and even dangerous to cross them. In attempting to get near some geese this day I sunk to the waist amidst snow and water, and not being able to get any firm footing, I found much difficulty in scrambling out without wetting my gun.

23rd.—This being a fine day, all the men were employed dismantling the house and carrying down the provisions, clothes, &c. to the summer tents, which had been pitched about 300 yards nearer the shore. Two leather tents were put up for cooking in. We saw the sun at midnight, his lower limb touching the high grounds to the northward.

We made some bread in an oven which we had built of stones cemented with clay of an excellent quality. The upper part of our first batch was well baked, but the floor of the oven was not sufficiently warm to bake the lower part. It however rose well, and we afterwards succeeded in making excellent bread, though the oven was heated with heather.*

15th July.—Weather still stormy and cold to the feelings, the thermometer being +35°. The water of North Pole Lake had broken through its barrier of

---

* Receipt.—Seven lbs. flour, 1 oz. carbonate soda, ¾ oz. citric acid, ¾ oz. common salt, water (cold), about ½ gallon. The salt, soda, and acid being finely powdered and dry, are to be well mixed together; this mixture being well wrought up with the dry flour, the water is to be added in 2 or 3 parts and mingled with the flour as quickly as possible; the dough being put into pans is immediately to be placed in the oven.

snow and ice, and was rushing down the river with great force, carrying with it large masses of ice.

All the men except Flett, who remained at the tents, and Germain, who had charge of the nets, went to North Pole Lake on the 19th to bring down the boat. The river being one continued rapid throughout its whole length, with not an eddy to stop in, they came down at rather a quick-rate, but were compelled to stop within a few hundred yards of the salt water, on account of the shallowness and the number of stones. Twenty-two salmon were caught, some in good condition, others very soft and thin. The former contained roe about the eighth of an inch in diameter.

A number of Esquimaux arrived for the purpose of catching salmon, having finished their seal hunting, which had been successful, although the number killed could not be ascertained. Our old friends were accompanied by three strangers, viz., an old man and two young ones, with their wives and families. Our travelling companion Ivitchuk had shot some deer with his gun, but having spent nearly all his ammunition, he requested and obtained a small additional stock.

Another Esquimaux, a jolly old fellow, with two wives, joined the party here; he had come from the direction of Wager River this spring on the ice. He and one or two more old men were nearly starved to death last winter, being so much reduced that they could not walk. Twenty-three salmon were got

from the nets ; some of these were in very poor condition, being evidently out of season ; others were
in fine order and full of roe.

22nd.—One of the old Esquimaux at the fishery
speared a seal on the ice near the edge of the open
water, but it got away in consequence of the line
breaking. Their mode of approaching the seal requires much patience and is very fatiguing, as the
hunter must lie flat on his face or on his side, and
advance towards the seal by a series of motions
resembling those of the animal itself. He has frequently to proceed in this way some hundred yards,
but so well does he act his part that he can get
within a few feet of his object, and a looker-on
would find much difficulty in telling which was the
man and which the seal.

The seal actually comes to meet the hunter, who,
as soon as it has got some distance from its hole,
springs up and intercepts its return. The women
are very expert at this mode of hunting, and frequently having no spear, use a small club of wood
with which they strike the seal on the nose.

The greater part of the Esquimaux were encamped about a quarter of a mile from us, and had
a *concert* every night,—a union of the vocal and the
instrumental. Their only musical instrument is a
sort of drum or tambourine, consisting of a stout
wooden hoop, about 30 inches in diameter, round
which, when it is to be used, a wet parchment deer
skin is stretched. In beating this rough instrument,

the hoop, not the skin, is struck. The performer being in the centre of the tent, keeps turning slowly round, whilst four or five women add their voices to the execrable sound, producing among them most horrible discord. Each of the men in his turn takes up the drum and thumps away till he is tired, when he lays it down and another takes his place, and so on it goes until it has passed through the hands of all the males of the party, including the boys.

The whole of the natives, with the exception of a few old people who were remaining at the fishing station, and three young men and their wives, went the following day to an island four miles off for the purpose of killing more seals, and also to put new covers on their canoe frames.

25th.—This was the anniversary of our arrival here last year; and certainly everything wore a very different aspect from what it then did. Last summer at this date there was no ice to be seen in Repulse Bay ; the snow had nearly all disappeared, and the various streams had shrunk to their lowest level. *Now* there was not a pool of water in the bay, except where the entrance of a river or creek had worn away or broken up the ice for a short distance. There was much snow on the ground in many places, and most of the streams were still deep and rapid.

The musquitoes were rather troublesome ; but this I was not sorry for, as the Esquimaux said that the ice in the bay would soon break up after these tormentors made their appearance.

As our native friends were now getting sufficient fish to maintain them, they required no further assistance from us at present. Their mode of catching salmon is a very simple one. They build a barrier of stones about 1½ or 2 feet high across a creek, some distance below high-water mark. The salmon, which keep close to the shore at this season, are by this means, during the ebb of the tide, cut off from the sea, and are easily speared. About sixty were thus killed this day. The spear used is usually made of two diverging pieces of musk-ox horn, from 4 to 5 inches apart at the extremities; between these there is a prong of bone about 3 or 4 inches shorter than the outer ones. Each of the longer prongs is furnished with a barb on its inner side, made of a bent nail or piece of bone, which prevents the fish from escaping. The handle is 6 or 8 feet long. The head of the instrument much resembles a three-pronged fork, with the middle prong a little shorter than the others.

The moon was full this day. High-water at 45 minutes past noon. Arkshuk, Shimakuk, and Kei-ik-too-oo visited us on the 28th, bringing a few pairs of boots for sale. The tins which contained preserved meat, and table knives and forks, were in great demand among these good folks. One of the ladies to whom I gave a fork, used it as neatly in eating fish as if she had been accustomed to it from childhood. Thermometer as high as $+60°$ in the shade.

The ice in the bay had broken up for more than a mile from the shore opposite the mouth of the river, but some distance out it looked as white and firm as ever.

I had for some time observed that large stones, some of them of one or two tons weight, were making their appearance on the ice ; and I was much puzzled to make out how they came there. They could not have fallen from the shore, as the beach was sloping at the place, nor had they been carried in by drift ice of the previous season. The only way that I could account for it was this. At the commencement of winter the ice, after acquiring considerable thickness, had become frozen to the stones lying on the bottom, and raised them up when the tide came in. The stones would get gradually enclosed in the ice as it grew thicker by repeated freezings, whilst by the process of evaporation, which goes on very rapidly in the spring, the upper surface was continually wasting away, so that in June and July there was little of the first formed ice remaining, and thus the stones which at first were on the under surface of the ice appeared on the top. This may perhaps in some measure account for boulders, sand, shells, &c. being sometimes found where geologists fancy they ought not to be. Ice has been time out of mind the great " conveyancer."

August 1st.—We were visited this day by an Esquimaux named I-ik-tu-ang, whom I had not before seen. He had passed the winter near the

Ooglit Islands, a few days' journey from Igloolik. He said that, when a boy, he was frequently on board the Fury and Hecla in 1822–23, and that the " Kabloonans " killed a number of walruses, and some black whales, with two small boats; that the walruses were put in " cache " for them (the Esquimaux), who were rather short of provisions at the time, and that they received the *skins* of the whales. They had abundance of provisions last winter, but were visited by a very fatal disease—from what I learnt of the symptoms, resembling influenza—which carried off twenty-one grown-up persons. The children were not attacked with this complaint. Two of the party at Igloolik had been reduced to the necessity of putting to death and eating two children, to save themselves from starvation.

Four men, whilst hunting the sea-horse with their canoes lashed together, were assaulted by this fierce animal, struck down with his formidable tusks, their canoes capsized and broken, and the whole party drowned. Another poor fellow having early in the winter harpooned a walrus through a hole in the ice, was dragged into the water before he could disengage himself from the line. The ice being still thin and transparent, the body was found a few days after.

I-ik-tu-ang also informed me—as I had already supposed from various appearances—that there is open water throughout the winter between this and the Frozen Strait, through which a strong current runs with the flow and ebb of the tide,—so strong is it that when bears are pursued and take the water, they are often swept under the ice and drowned.

In the afternoon two more Esquimaux with their wives from the same quarter, accompanied by Akkee-ou-lik and his family, made their appearance.

Some of the natives who had taken up their quarters near us were supplied daily with fish. They appeared quite as indolent as most of the other savage tribes of America, and never thought of looking out for food, so long as they could get enough to support life from us. Although they had a wear made for confining the salmon, they would not take the trouble to spear them when in it.

We endeavoured to get some young marmots, but without success. I find that these curious little animals leave their winter habitations, which are usually formed in dry sandy banks, as soon as the snow has in a great measure disappeared, and take up their summer residence among the rocks, where, I have no doubt, they are much safer from their numerous enemies.

The weather was still fine on the 6th, but it appeared to have little effect on the ice in the bay, which still remained hard and fast. All the largest and deepest lakes were covered with strong ice.

9th.—On looking out this morning I was happy to see a lane of open water stretching completely across the bay, but there was still a strong barrier between us and the south point, although a passage to the northward might easily have been made. The nets produced eighty salmon, the greater part of which were given to the Esquimaux. The fishery was now abandoned, as we could procure close at hand as many salmon as we required.

During the whole of our spring fishing Halkett's air-boat was used for setting and examining the nets, and was preferred by the fishermen to the large canvas canoe, as it was much lighter, and passed over and round the nets with more facility. Notwithstanding its continued use on a rocky shore, it never required the slightest repair. It is altogether a most useful little vessel, and, as I have said before, ought to form part of the equipment of all surveying parties, whether by land or sea.

The men from the fishery were followed soon after by the Esquimaux with their baggage, which it took more than a dozen trips of our canoe to ferry over.

The large lakes were still covered with a thick coat of ice. There were a great many seals in the open water, and some of the fish in the nets had been eaten by them.

10th.—A storm from the north with rain and snow until noon, when the wind somewhat abated, and the weather cleared up. Great havoc was made among the ice, and in the evening there was a clear sea as far as the point of the bay.

11th.—There was a gale of wind all day with rain occasionally—the weather cold and unpleasant.

We were all busily employed in preparing for sea. All the snow-banks for six or eight feet from the ground having been converted into solid ice soon after the spring thaw commenced, we had to dig out the chain and anchor of one of the boats, which were buried under ice of that thickness; yet on the very spot where this chain and anchor lay, there was not a particle of either ice or snow on the 25th July last year; such is the variable nature of this northern climate.

In the afternoon Nibitabo was sent to endeavour to get some fresh venison for our voyage, and shot two young deer; St. Germain and Mineau set the nets for a supply of salmon, and I was busy distributing among the Esquimaux axes, files, knives, scissors, &c. &c. &c.

The large lakes were still covered with ice, but in the bay there was little or none to be seen.

CHAPTER IX.

Voyage from Repulse Bay to York Factory.

HAVING got every thing ready, the boat launched and loaded about 2 o'clock P.M. on the 12th of August, I was about to distribute our spare kettles, some hoop iron, &c. among the Esquimaux, when the compass of one of the boats was missing. Search was made, but no compass was to be found. At last I thought of turning over some heather that lay close to where my tent had been, and there discovered it. It had been concealed by one of the Esquimaux women —a widow—to whom more presents had been made than to any ofvthe others.

Some of the most decent of the men appeared really sorry at parting, and waded into the water to shake hands with me.

We got under weigh with a light air of wind from the N.E. at 25 minutes past 2. Our progress was very slow, there being frequent calms, so that, between pulling and sailing, we reached only to within five miles of Cape Hope at 4 A.M. of the

13th. A large black whale and some white ones, with innumerable seals, were seen. Thermometer at + 65 ; but it became much colder after the wind came from sea. During the night we sailed among loose ice. As it was still calm we anchored at half-past 4 A.M. to wait for the other boat, which was some miles astern, to re-stow the cargo and cook breakfast. Thermometer at 5 A.M. + 48°.

At half-past 6 we began pulling along shore. An hour afterwards a light breeze sprung up, but still ahead. The breeze becoming stronger, we hoisted sail and turned to windward, and would have made good progress had it kept steady ; instead of which it followed or rather preceded the sun in his course westward, and thus headed us at every point we weathered. The flood-tide assisted us until 4 P.M., when we put ashore, as the ebb was too strong for us. Shot a young Arctic hare. There is a number of long narrow lakes near the point we stopped at, which is formed of grey and red granite and gneiss, and is about five miles from the S.E. point of Repulse Bay. Caught three species of marine insects with fins, which they use like wings : preserved specimens of them. Every appearance of rain this evening. Thermometer + 65° at 8 P.M.

14th. The wind shifted to the N.N.W. at half-past 9 last night, when we immediately got under weigh and sailed cautiously along shore, examining every bay and inlet when I supposed us near the northern outlet of Wager River, but not a trace of it was to be seen. If it exists, I think it not likely that it should have escaped our notice twice. The wind was for a few hours variable and squally; but it now shifted to N.E. by N. and blew hard. In crossing Wager River Bay, eight or ten miles from shore, there was a very heavy cross sea, which washed over our gunwales occasionally. On nearing the shore the run of the sea became more regular; but the wind increased so as to make it necessary to reef sails. The weather assuming a very threatening appearance, and the navigation being intricate and dangerous, we were forced to seek a harbour, which, after some difficulty, we found in a small bay at 8 P.M., having run from ninety to ninety-five miles, seventy-three of which were measured by Massey's patent log. Two white bears and many walruses were seen on a small island near Whale Island; but the weather was too stormy to permit us to pursue them.

It had been my intention to cross over to Southampton Island and trace that portion of the coast from Port Harding southward which had not yet been surveyed; but a stream of ice and the state of the weather prevented my doing so, nor did I think it an object of sufficient importance to detain the expedition a day or two for that sole purpose. Thermometer about + 41° all day.

The male eider and king ducks appeared to have

left this coast already, there being none but females seen. Our boat took the ground about half ebb— a fine bottom of sand and mud.

15th. It blew a complete gale all night and during the greater part of this day. The sky, however, was sufficiently clear to allow me to obtain a meridian observation for latitude and variation. The former was found to be 64° 49' 06″ N. — the latter 41° 27' W. Thermometer + 46°.

The wind began to fall in the evening, and the tide having come in so as to float the boats, we started at 4 p.m. under reefed sails. The sea was still running high, but it was long and regular; and as there was every appearance of fine weather, I determined to sail all night, keeping a sharp look-out ahead for shoals, reefs, and islets. There was a heavy swell all night which broke with great violence on the reefs; and it being very dark, both boats were once or twice nearly filled by getting into shallow water before we were aware of it.

16th. At half-past 5 this morning we were opposite Cape Fullerton, and at 6 Massey's log was examined, when it indicated a run of seventy-two miles. At 9 a.m. it fell calm. Thermometer +43°. An hour afterwards there was a light breeze from S.W., with which we turned to windward among numerous rocky islands.

At noon the latitude, 63° 56' 13″ N., was observed, and shortly afterwards two Esquimaux were seen coming off in their kayaks, paddling at a great rate;

but the breeze had now freshened, and it would have given them hard work to overtake us had we not shortened sail, and afterwards landed on an island, where we waited for them. Three more joined us there. They were very dirty, and far inferior in every respect to our friends of Repulse Bay. One of them was about five feet eight inches high, had a formidable beard and moustache, and was better looking than the others. After making them some presents we shoved off, and stood across the bay to the westward of Cape Fullerton. This bay is much deeper than it is laid down in the chart, and is crowded with islands.

It was near high water when we reached the main shore, and as we could make no progress against wind and tide, we put into a safe harbour. Nothing was to be seen for a mile or two inland but rocks, clothed in some spots with moss or grass. Deer were observed, and a young one shot by Nibitabo.

About an hour after our landing the wind shifted to W.N.W., and, as I was afraid of getting aground in our present berth, the boats were moved to a more open situation from which they could start at any time of tide.

The Esquimaux could tell us nothing about Churchill, none of them having visited that place either this or the previous summer. Thermometer at 9 P.M. +53.

17th.—We were under weigh at 2 A.M., but the

wind was both light and close, so that our progress was slow. Before the tide changed it came more from the southward; we were therefore obliged to anchor as soon as it began to ebb. The latitude of our harbour was 63° 47′ 33″ N. Var. 31° 8′ W. The rocks, like those where we landed last night, were grey granite and gneiss. Thermometer at noon +60°. A large black whale was seen this morning.

At half-past 1 P.M. the tide began to flow, and at two we were under sail, the wind having gone round to the northward, so as to permit us to lie our course along shore. A succession of reefs lines the coast, which is itself very irregular in its outline, being indented with numberless inlets, some of them running many miles inland.

The tide began to ebb at 8 P.M., and as the wind had fallen and headed us, we ran in shore and cast anchor under the shelter of some rocks. It was just getting dark when a fresh breeze of fair wind sprung up. This was annoying enough. At 10 o'clock nine Esquimaux visited us, but staid only a short time, as we were to stop near their tents in the morning. Two of them said they would sleep on the rocks near us, with the intention of pointing out the deepest channel when we should resume our voyage.

18th.—We started at daylight this morning, but the fair wind, which had continued all night, soon failed us. Aided by the flood-tide, however, an hours rowing brought us to the encampment of our last night's visitors, who welcomed us with much noise, and soon brought to the beach a number of furs and other articles for trade. They were very easy to deal with, apparently putting implicit confidence in our honesty ; nor were they losers by this conduct. Ammunition was the article chiefly in demand, as they had two guns among the party. Files, knives, fire-steels, &c. were distributed among the men, and beads, needles, buttons, &c. among the women. One of the women was rather good-looking, but they were all much darker than the natives of Repulse Bay. They were well provided with food, as they had a large seal lying on the rocks, besides venison. It was still calm when we left them, but favoured by the ebb-tide we pulled out of the inlet, and shaped our course towards Chesterfield Inlet, which we crossed with the last of the flood. The day was beautiful—far too much so— and the few light airs of wind were all against us. We landed in a small cove on the south side of the inlet to pick up a deer that was shot from the boat. Four more deer were killed, but all in poor condition.

About two miles to the northward of the inlet I obtained a meridian observation of the sun in the natural horizon, which gave latitude 63° 32′ 00″ N. Thermometer at noon +65°, and in the evening

+70°. The musquitoes were very numerous and troublesome. Numbers of turnstones (*Tringa interpres*) were seen.

19th.—There was a fine breeze again all last night, which died away at daylight. As soon as the flood-tide began to come in, we started with a light wind fair enough to allow us to lie our course along shore for a few miles. It again fell calm, when we took to the oars and landed on a point five miles to the southward of our last night's harbour, where we breakfasted at 9 A.M.

Dovekies in countless numbers were sitting on the stones, and swimming along the shore;* one or two pintailed and mallard ducks were seen on a lake a few hundred yards inland—the first we have seen since passing Nevill's Bay last year. Some dovekies' eggs were found with the birds formed in them.

Having obtained a meridian observation of the sun, which gave for the latitude 63° 17' 00″ N., and variation 9° 21' W., we got under weigh and beat to windward with the last of the ebb, which here ran to the south. There was a fine breeze, but we made only about five miles southing, when at 6 P.M.

---

* The dovekie, or black guillemot (*Uria grylle*), breeds in great numbers in the Orkney islands. I believe ornithologists are mistaken in supposing that this bird becomes white or rather grey during the winter. It is only the young birds that are so; the old ones are seen in winter without any change in the colour of their summer plumage.

the flood setting in strong against us, we put ashore
for the night under the lee of the point. It was
not easy to find a harbour, all the coast from
Chesterfield Inlet being flat and stony, and lined
with shoals. A young buck was shot, but it was
in poor condition. Thermometer at noon +63°
—at 8 P.M. +57°. Some of the copper came off
our boat to-day and stopped her way before it was
observed.

20th.—We were under weigh this morning by
daylight, but the wind was right ahead and blowing
fresh. Some more copper came off the boat, and
she was evidently out of trim, as the Magnet went
fast to windward of us. She had become leaky
also, and therefore I determined to lay her aground
as soon as the tide turned.

We had gained between six and seven miles,
when, finding that we made but slow progress, I
put on shore at the first place that offered shelter,
a little before noon. Several deer were seen, and a
large buck shot, which I was surprised to find very
lean. At this season, near Repulse Bay they are
in fine condition. Thermometer at noon +61°. At
half-past 2 the wind changed to W.N.W., but it
blew a gale before the tide flowed sufficiently to
float us. We could do nothing but haul out into
deeper water, to be ready by dawn next morning.

Some pintails, mallards, and Hutchins and
laughing geese were seen here; also a brood of
well-grown young king-ducks in a small lake at

some distance from the sea, with which it had no connection.

Just as our boats floated, the wind became more moderate ; and as we had still an hour and a half of daylight, we sailed along the coast for 4½ miles, being forced to keep some miles from shore to avoid shoals. Soon after sunset we ran into a bay for shelter during the night. In doing so we grazed some ridges of stones, but found good anchorage in four fathoms water. Thermometer +47°.

21st.—Thermometer +44°. There was a strong breeze with heavy squalls from the north all night. On starting at daylight and making for the only outlet that appeared, we found it too shallow, and so were forced to wait the flow of the tide. The wind was W. by N., but gradually shifted round against us and became very light. We managed, however, to reach an island near the north point of Rankin's Inlet.

Although there was a fine breeze, it being right ahead, nothing was to be gained against the ebb tide.

We found many old signs of Esquimaux visits to the island. Among other articles picked up were an ivory snow-knife, a drill for producing fire, and an iron drill ; also some vertebræ of a whale measuring ten inches in diameter. There were numerous graves of Esquimaux here, with spears, lances, &c. deposited beside them. Most of these articles were old and much corroded with rust, but a very excellent seal-spear head had been placed there this spring. Thermometer at noon +52°; 8 P.M. +47°. Temperature of water +41°.

22nd.—Thermometer +42°. At a little before 5 this morning the wind shifted to S.S.E. We set out to cross Rankin's Inlet, although we could not lie our course, and after five hours' sailing reached an island near the south shore, where we landed, as the breeze had increased to a gale and gone more to the southward, with a heavy sea, which washed over us occasionally. We here picked up some specimens of copper ore, but the ore did not appear to be abundant.

The aurora was very bright last night. It appeared first to the S.S.E., moved rapidly northward, spreading all over the sky, and finally disappearing in the north. This agrees with what Wrangel asserts, " that the aurora is affected by the wind in the same way as clouds are." Heavy rain and a strong gale from noon until 8 P.M. Temperature of water +42°; air +43°.

23rd.—The wind was right ahead but light this morning. We got under weigh and beat to windward some miles, alternately sailing and pulling until we reached the north point of Corbett's Inlet. We were here visited by eighteen Esquimaux in their kayaks. All the news they could give us was that one of Ouligbuck's sons had passed the winter near this place, and that he had walked to Churchill in the winter, where all were then well. A brisk trade was soon opened; the articles in greatest request being powder and ball. Some fox and wolf skins were received; but before they had brought out the half of their stock, the wind changed from S.W. to N.W. by W. and blew a gale, which soon raised a sea that washed over the canoes alongside. Being anxious to take advantage of the fair wind to cross Corbett's Inlet before dark, after making our friends presents of various articles, we set sail and ran across the inlet, encountering a heavy sea caused by a swell from the south meeting the waves raised by the present gale. We were three hours crossing to the south point of the inlet, off which lie some dangerous reefs five or six miles from land. The wind was very close as we turned the point; and after gaining six miles further, we were forced to make a number of tacks before getting into a harbour, which proved to be an excellent one, land-locked on all sides. Little soil was to be seen on the rocks, which were of granite. We had shipped a good deal of water, and it was past 9 P.M. when we got under shelter. Thermometer +45°. Hundreds of grey phalaropes were seen, supposed to be Phalaropus fulicarius.

24th.—It blew so hard this morning that we could not start until 8 o'clock. The wind after that moderated gradually, and latterly fell calm. By

rowing we arrived at the S.E. end of the island *
near Whale Cove, where we were visited by a party
of natives, who brought off some furs and boots for
trade. A breeze from S.S.E. sprung up about
1 o'clock, with which we turned to windward
through a narrow channel between a small island
and the main. When we reached the open sea the
wind was too much ahead for us to advance against
the ebb tide, and as a convenient harbour offered
itself, we anchored for the night. Our latitude at
noon was 62° 13′ 19″; after which we advanced
about four miles to the southward. Ouligbuck told
us that, when a little boy about seven years old,
he visited this place with his parents, and went out
to Sea-Horse Island on the ice to hunt the animals
from which it takes its name. Three large black
whales were seen to-day. Thermometer +46°,
+53°, and +42°.

I was much pleased to observe that the nearer we
approached to Churchill, the more confidence the
Esquimaux placed in us. They fixed no price for
their goods, but threw them on board the boat, and
left it to me to pay them what I pleased. This
confidential mode of dealing, which is not in keeping with the habits of the Esquimaux tribes, at least
shows that they are satisfied with the treatment they
receive at Churchill. To the Hudson's Bay Company, indeed, they have much reason to be grateful

* This place is laid down on the chart as an island, but is a peninsula according to the account we received from the Esquimaux.

for having, by their influence, at last created a friendly feeling between them and the Chipewyans, with whom they used to be at constant and deadly enmity.

25th. — There was heavy rain all last night, which continued until between 9 and 10 o'clock this morning. We then got under weigh with the first of the flood, but it fell calm. We rowed for fourteen or fifteen miles, the rain pouring all the time. A fine breeze from N. by E. sprung up at 4 P.M., before which we ran direct for the passage between Sir Bibye's Islands ; but finding the water become very shallow, and learning from Ouligbuck that there was not water enough for boats except at full tide, we kept outside the islands altogether. We reached the main land a little after sunset at the south point of Nevill's Bay, and ran for shelter into a small inlet separated on the south by a narrow point from a deep river, to which the Esquimaux resort to catch salmon. Thermometer +37° and +41°. As the moon was full, I at first intended running on all night, but the threatening look of the weather deterred me.

26th.—Last night, about an hour after casting anchor, the moon became overcast, and it blew a perfect gale. On landing this morning we found a quantity of wood, a large sledge 30 feet long, and some slender pieces of wood fastened together to the length of 40 feet. There were two of these poles, which are used by the natives for spearing small

192

seals. It is said that, in Davis' Straits, the Esquimaux use poles of the same kind for spearing whales.

As the bay in which we were lying was not very safe should the wind change, we got under weigh and turned into the mouth of the river under close-reefed sails. The boats shipped much water, particularly the Magnet, keeping a man constantly baling. We at last got under the lee of a point where there was a sandy bottom, but not water enough to float the boats at low tide. The river is about a mile broad, and deep enough in the middle for a vessel drawing 12 or 14 feet water.

We saw a number of whalebone snares set along the edges of the lakes for geese, large flocks of which were feeding about, but very shy. There was a storm from N.N.W. all the afternoon with heavy rain. Thermometer +36°.

27th.—It felt very cold this morning; the thermometer was at the freezing point, and there was some snow. The storm had continued all night with increasing strength, but towards day-light the weather became more moderate, so that about 9 o'clock we were able to start under reefed sails. The breeze gradually died away and went round to the S.W., and it finally became calm. Heavy rain and sleet began to fall; the wind veered round to the S.E., so that we could lie our course, and make good progress with the flood.

At 6 P.M. we reached a bay a few miles north of Knapp's Bay, which I had not noticed on our outward voyage, and which is not laid down on the charts. It is about ten miles wide and eight deep; the water in it is very shallow, no where exceeding ten feet; and as it was within an hour or two of high water, the greater part of it must be dry when the tide is out.

Numbers of Brent geese were feeding in all directions on a marine plant *(zostera marina*, Linn.) which grows here in great abundance.

We anchored under the lee of an islet in Knapp's Bay, a very small portion of which was visible at high water. Thermometer +38°.

28th.—We were under weigh at day-light this morning, with a strong breeze of north-west wind, which made us close-reef our sails. There was a heavy sea in Knapp's Bay. At 8 A.M. we passed to the westward of the island, under which we found shelter during the gale of the 8th of July last. The wind was cold, with occasional showers of rain. Great numbers of geese were seen passing to the southward. In the evening the wind became more moderate and finally calm. Our water-kegs being empty, I ran inshore a little before sunset, and entered Egg River, in which we found a safe harbour. This river discharges a considerable body of water into the sea by five mouths, separated by four islets. There is no island lying opposite to its mouth, as represented in the charts. Thermometer from +35° to +40°.

29th.—The boat lay afloat all the night, which

was fine but dark. There was not a breath of wind until 7 o'clock. An hour after starting, a moderate breeze sprung up from W. by N., but soon became light and variable, and at last it fell calm a short time before sunset, when, having gained about 40 miles, we pulled into a small bay, which afforded us good shelter. The day was fine throughout, with occasional light showers of rain. Thermometer from $+45°$ to $+52°$.

The sky was too much overcast for me to obtain any observation, but it appears to me that Egg River is laid down in the charts about 12 miles too far to the southward, and Egg Island is 12 miles south of the river instead of being near its mouth, as there represented.

30th.—We had 13 feet water last night when the tide was in, but it was not until the flood had made two hours that we floated. The night was as fine as the last and calm. There was a light air of west wind when we got under weigh, with which and the flood-tide we slipped alongshore pretty fast. In an hour or two the wind began to fly about from all points, with calms between, so that even with the help of our oars we only made 22 miles; and not being able to reach Seal River, we ran into a small bay—the only spot that appeared clear of stones for some miles—about 12 miles north of it. Here abundance of drift wood was found, with which the men lighted fires sufficiently large for the coldest winter night. The evening was very warm, and the musquitoes were troublesome. The country inland is well wooded. Great numbers of mallard, teal, pintails, and long-tailed ducks were seen, but only two or three were shot.

31st.—Left our harbour as soon as the tide permitted, which was at 7 A.M. A light but fair breeze from N. by W. gradually increased, so that we made a fine run across Button's Bay, which is as full of rocks and shoals as represented in the charts, and entering Churchill River a few minutes after 1 P.M., landed in a small cove a few hundred yards above the Old Fort.

On visiting the Company's establishment, I found that Mr. Sinclair was absent at York Factory; but I was very kindly received by Mrs. Sinclair, and liberally supplied with everything we required for the continuation of our voyage. As we had carried away our bowsprit, Turner was set to make a new one.

I received many letters from much valued friends, and after remaining for a few hours, returned to the boats at 9 P.M. in order to be prepared for starting early in the morning, should wind and weather prove favourable. The stock of provisions on hand was eight bags of pemmican and four cwt. of flour. We left Ouligbuck and his son at Churchill.

3rd September.—For the last two days the wind had been fair, but blowing a gale, with such a heavy sea that we could not proceed. The weather was so cloudy that I could obtain no observations;

I therefore employed most of my time in shooting Esquimaux curlews, which were so abundant near the Old Fort that I bagged seven brace in a few hours.

This morning the wind shifted more to the westward, and becoming more moderate, we got under weigh at 9 A.M. There was still a heavy swell outside and at the entrance of our little harbour. Whilst coming out in the dawn of the morning three seas came rolling in one after the other, and broke completely over the bows of the boat, washing her from stem to stern. I thought she would have filled, but we got into deep water before any more seas caught her. The Magnet was even more roughly handled in following us, having shipped much water and struck heavily on the rocks—fortunately without damage. The wind died away, and during the morning shifted to south. We, however, reached Cape Churchill, and at 8 P.M. cast anchor under its lee, exactly opposite an old stranded boat.

4th.—We had a breeze from S. W. by S. to-day, which enabled us to get along the coast sixteen or eighteen miles during the flood. It blew so hard in the afternoon that we required to double-reef our sails. The weather was very warm, the thermometer being as high as $+ 60°$ in the shade. A Canada nuthatch *(sitta Canadensis)* flew on board to-day, and was very nearly caught. There were a good many ducks and geese near the place where we landed to get fresh water. Between thirty and forty of the former and two of the latter were shot. The boats were allowed to take the ground, after two hours' ebb, on a fine shingle beach, on which a considerable surf was breaking.

5th.—It was calm all night. At 3 this morning the boat floated, and we pushed out a short distance from shore to be ready for the first fair wind. At half-past seven a light air sprung up from N. E., but did not increase till past noon, when there was a fine breeze. A meridian observation of the sun gave latitude 58° 26′ 14″ N. At 5 P.M. we were opposite the mouth of Broad River, latitude 58° 7′ 0″ N. Thermometer at noon + 56°.

6th.—We were under weigh this morning a little before daylight with the wind from N. E. The weather was so thick that we could not see more than a hundred yards ahead. We, however, ran on by soundings until I thought we were near North River, and then kept inshore until we got sight of land, which proved to be close to Nelson River, across which we stood, directing our course by compass, and coming in directly opposite the beacon. We arrived at York Factory between 9 and 10 o'clock, P.M. and were warmly welcomed by our friends, who had not expected to see us until next summer.

In justice to the men under me, let me here express my thanks for their continued good conduct under circumstances sometimes sufficiently trying ;—

in fact, a better set of fellows it would be difficult to find anywhere.

As to their appearance when we arrived at York Factory, I may adopt the words of Corporal M'Laren in charge of the Sappers and Miners who are to accompany Sir John Richardson,—" By George, I never saw such a set of men."

APPENDIX.

LIST OF MAMMALIA,

Collected during Mr. Rae's Expedition, with Observations by J. E. Gray, Esq., F.R.S. &c.

1. *Mus Musculus.* Linn. York Factory. Probably introduced from Europe.
2. *Arctomys Parryi.* Richardson, Faun. Bor. Amer. p. 158, tab. 10.
3. *Lepus Glacialis.* Leach. Richardson, Faun. Bor. Amer. 221.

MYODES.—The specimens brought by the expedition have enabled me to make some corrections in the characters assigned to these species. I may observe that the large size or peculiar form of the claws which has been regarded as a character of the species, appears to be peculiar to one sex—probably the males.

   1. *The upper cutting teeth narrow, smooth without any longitudinal groove. Thumb with a compressed curved acute claw.* (Lemnus).

Myodes, Lemnus Pallas. Glires 77 of Sweden.

Myodes Helvolus. Richardson, Faun. Bor. Amer. p. 128, belong to this section. All the museum specimens of these species have small, simple, curved, acute claws.

4. *Myodes Hudsonius.* Richardson, Faun. Bor. Amer. 132.

Grey, black washed beneath white, sides reddish, sides of the neck red, nose with a central black streak, claws of male (?) very large, compressed, equal, broad to the end, and notched; of female small, acute. In winter with very long black white-tipped hairs. Mr. Rae brought home two males, one in winter and one in change fur, and two females in summer fur.

5. *Myodes Greenlandicus.*

Reddish-grey, brown, black varied, back with a longitudinal black streak, beneath grey brown, chest, nape, and sides ruffous. Front claw of males (?) compressed, curved, the under surface (especially of the middle one) with a broad, round, expanded tubercle. I have not seen this species showing any change in its winter fur.

2. *Upper cutting teeth broader, with a central longitudinal groove. The claw of the front thumb strap-shaped, truncated, and notched at the tip.*

6. *Myodes Helvolus.* Richardson, Faun. Bor. Amer. 128. (female?)

Fur very long, black, grey-brown; black grizzled, hinder part of the body reddish, beneath grey, sides yellowish. Claws of the fore feet (of the males?) large, 'thick, rounded, curved, bluntly truncated at the tip; of the female compressed, curved, acute.

7. *Myodes Trimuconatus.* Richardson, Faun. Bor. Amer. 130.

Bright red brown, head blackish-grey, sides and beneath pale ruffous, chin white, claws moderate, compressed. This species is best distinguished from the former by its larger size and the great brightness of the colour, and the fur being much shorter and less fluffly.

LIST OF THE SPECIES OF BIRDS

Collected by Mr. Rae during his late Expedition, named according to the " Fauna Boreali-Americana," by G. R. Gray, Esq., F.L.S.

FALCONIDÆ.
Aquila (Pandion) haliæeta.
Falco peregrinus.
    „   islandicus.
Accipiter (Astur) palumbarius.
Buteo lagopus.
    „   (Circus) cyaneus.
STRIGIDÆ.
Strix brachyota.
    „   funerea.
    „   Tengmalmi.
JANIADÆ.
Tyrannula pusilla.
MERULIDÆ.
Merula solitaria.
SYLVIADÆ.
Svlvicola æstiva.
    „   coronata.

Sylvicola striata.

   ,,   (Vermivora) rubricapilla.

   ,,   ,,   peregrina.

Seiurius aquaticus.

Anthus aquaticus.

FRINGILLIDÆ.

Alauda cornuta.

Emberiza (Plectrophanes) nivalis.

   ,,   ,,   lapponica.

   ,,   ,,   picta.

   ,,   canadensis

   ,,   (Zonotrichia) leucophrys.

   ,,   ,,   pennsylvanica.

   ,,   ,,   iliaca.

Fringilla hyemalis.

Pyrrhula (Corythus) enucleator.

Logia leucoptera.

Linaria minor.

STURNIDÆ.

Quiscalus versicolor.

Scolecophagus ferrugineus.

CORVIDÆ.

Garrulus canadensis.

PICIDÆ.

Picus (Apternus) tridactylus.

Colaptes auratus.

RASORES.

Tetrao canadensis.

   ,,   (Lagopus) mutus.

   ,,   ,,   saliceti.

   ,,   (Centrocercus) phasianellus.

GRALLATORES.

Calidris arenaria.

Charadrius semipalmata.

Vanellus melanogaster.
Strepsilas interpres.
Tringa Douglassii.
    ,,   maritima.
    ,,   alpina.
    ,,   Schinzii.
    ,,   pusilla.
    ,,   cinerea.
Totanus flavipes.
    ,,   macularius.
Limosa hudsonica.
Scolopax Wilsoni.
Phalaropus hyperboreus
    ,,   fulicarius.
NATATORES.
Podiceps cornutus.
Larus argentatoides.
Lestris pomarina.
    ,,   parasitica.
    ,,   Richardsoni.
Anas (Boschas) crecca, var.
    ,,   ,,   discors.
Somateria spectabilis.
    ,,   mollissima.
Oidemia perspicillata.
    ,,   americana.
Harelda glacialis.
Mergus serrator.
Anser albifrons.
    ,,   hyperboreus.
    ,,   Hutchinsii.
    ,,   bernicla.
Colymbus arcticus.
    ,,   septentrionalis.

Myiodioctes pusilla.
Regulus calendula.
Sitta canadensis.
Linaria borealis.
Tringa rufescens.
    ,,   pectoralis.
Totanus solitarius.

FISHES,

Collected during Mr. Rae's Expedition. **By J. E. Gray,**
Esq., F.R.S.

GADIDÆ.

Lota Maculosus. Richardson, Faun. Bor. Amer.
iii. 248. Male and female.

ESOCIDÆ.

Esox. Lucius. Richardson, Faun. Bor. Amer. iii. 124.
Female.

CYPRINIDÆ.

Catastomus Forsterianus? Richardson, Faun. Bor.
Amer. iii. 116. Female. Lakes near York Factory. The "Red Sucker."

Catastomus Hudsonius. Richardson, Faun. Bor.
Amer. iii. 112. River near York Factory. "The
Grey Sucker."

SALMONIDÆ.

Salmo. Salar?? Richardson, Faun. Bor. Amer. 145.
Repulse Bay.

Salmo Hoodii. Richardson, Faun. Bor. Amer. iii.
173, t. 82, f. 2, t. 83, f. 2, t. 87, f. 1. Male and
female. Lakes near York Factory.

Salmo Coregonus Albus. Richardson, Faun. Bor.
Amer. 195. t. 89, f. 2. a. b. Male. The Atti-

hawmeg. Lower jaw shortest; ridge behind the eye becoming close to the orbit beneath the eye. *Salmo (Coregonus) Tullibee.* Richardson, Faun. Bor. Amer. 201. Lakes near York Factory. " The Tullibee." Lower jaw shortest, ridge behind continued distant from the orbit and produced towards the nostrils. *Salmo Coregonus Harengus?* Richardson, Faun. Bor. Amer. 210. t. 90, f. 2, a. b. Lower jaw longest, ridge behind the eyes becoming rather nearer to, but distinct from, the orbit beneath. River near York Factory.

PLANTS,
Named by Sir W. J. Hooker, K.H., D.C.L., F.R.A.& L.S. &c. &c. &c.

Plants collected on the Coast between York Factory *and* Churchill, *and in the neighbourhood of Churchill.*

DICOTYLEDONES.

Ranunculaceæ, *Juss.*
1. Anemone *Richardsoni,* Hook. Fl. Bor. Am. i. 6, Tab. 4, A.
2. Ranunculus *Lapponicus, L.*—Hook. Fl. Bor. Am. i. p. 16.

Cruciferæ, *Juss.*
3. Nasturtium *palustre,* De Cand.—Hook. Fl. Bor. Am. i. p. 39.
4. Arabis *petræa,* Lam.—Hook. Fl. Bor. Am. i. p. 42.
5. Cardamine *pratensis,* L.—Hook. Fl. Bor. Am. i. p. 45.
6. Draba *hirta,* L.—Hook. Fl. Bor. Am. i. p. 52.

7. Draba *alpina*, L.—Hook. Fl. Bor. Am. i. p. 50.

CARYOPHYLLEÆ, *Juss.*

8. Stellaria *Edwardsii*, Br.—Hook. Fl. Bor. Am. i. p. 96, Tab. 31.

9. Cerastium *alpinum*, L.—Hook. Fl. Bor. Am. i. p. 104.

10. Silene *acaulis*, L.—Hook. Fl. Bor. Am. i. p. 87.

11. Arenaria *peploides*, L.—Hook. Fl. Bor. Am. i. p. 102.

LEGUMINOSÆ, *Juss.*

12. Phaca *astragalina*, De Cand.—Hook. Fl. Bor. Am. i. p. 145.

13. Oxytropis *campestris*, De Cand.—Hook. Fl. Bor. Am. i. p. 147.

14. Oxytropis *deflexa*, De Cand.—Hook. Fl. Bor. Am. i. p. 148.

15. Hedysarum *Mackenzii*, Rich.—Hook. Fl. Bor. Am. i. p. 155.

ROSACEÆ, *Juss.*

16. Dryas *integrifolia*, Vahl,—Hook. Ex. Fl. Tab. 200, Fl. Bor. Am. i. p. 174.

17. Rubus *acaulis*, Mich.—Hook. Fl. Bor. Am. i. p. 182.

18. Potentilla *anserina*, L.—Hook. Fl. Bor. Am. i. p. 189.

19. Potentilla *pulchella*, Br.—Hook. Fl. Bor. Am. i. p. 191.

20. Potentilla *nivea*, L.—Hook. Fl. Bor. Am. i. p. 195.

ONAGRARIEÆ, *Juss.*

21. Epilobium *latifolium*, L.—Hook. Fl. Bor. Am. i. p. 205.

SAXIFRAGEÆ, *Juss.*

22. Saxifraga *oppositifolia*, L.—Hook. Fl. Bor. Am. i. p. 242.

23. Saxifraga *cæspitosa*, L.—Hook. Fl. Bor. Am. i. p. 244.

24. Saxifraga *Hirculus*, L.—Hook. Fl. Bor. Am. i. p. 252.

25. Saxifraga *tricuspidata*, L.—Hook. Fl. Bor. Am. i. p. 254.

COMPOSITÆ, *Juss.*

26. Nardosmia *corymbosa*, Hook. Fl. Bor. Am. i. p. 307 (Tussilago corymbosa, Br.)

27. Achillæa *millefolium*, L.—Hook. Fl. Bor. Am. i. p. 318.

28. Chrysanthemum *arcticum*, L.—Hook. Fl. Bor. Am. i. p. 319.

29. Pyrethrum *inodorum*, Sm. — Hook. Fl. Bor. Am. i. p. 320.

30. Senecio *aureus*, L.—Hook. Fl. Bor. Am. i. p. 333. var. nanus.

31. Arnica *montana*, L.—β. *angustifolia*, Hook. Fl. Bor. Am. i. p. 330.

CAMPANULACEÆ, *Juss.*

32. Campanula *uniflora*, L.—Hook. Fl. Bor. Am. ii. p. 29.

ERICEÆ, *L.*

33. Ledum *palustre*, L.—Hook. Fl. Bor. Am. ii. p. 44. —var. *a. angustifolium;* and var. *β. latifolium.*

34. Azalea *procumbens*, L.—Hook. Fl. Bor. Am. ii. p. 44.

35. Rhododendron *Lapponicum*, Wahl.—Hook. Fl. Bor. Am. ii. p. 43.

36. Vaccinium *Vitis Idæa*, L. — Hook. Fl. Bor. Am. ii. p. 34.

MONOTROPEÆ, *Nutt.*

37. Pyrola *rotundifolia*, L.—Hook. Fl. Bor. Am. ii. p. 46.

BORAGINEÆ, *Juss.*

38. Lithospermum *maritimum,* Lehm.—Hook. Fl. Bor. Am. ii. p. 86.

SCROPHULARINEÆ, *Juss.*

39. Castilleja *pallida,* Benth.—Hook. Fl. Bor. Am. ii. p. 105.

40. Bartsia *alpina,* L.—Hook. Fl. Bor. Am. ii. p. 106.

41. Pedicularis *Wlassoviana,* Stev.—Hook. Fl. Bor. Am. ii. p. 107.

42. Pedicularis *Lapponica,* L.—Hook. Fl. Am. ii. p. 108.

43. Pedicularis *Sudetica,* Willd.—Hook. Fl. Bor. Am. ii. p. 109.

44. Pedicularis *flammea,* L.—Hook. Fl. Bor. Am. ii. p. 110.

45. Pedicularis *euphrasioides,* Stev.—Hook. Fl. Bor. Am. ii. p. 108.

PRIMULACEÆ, *Juss.*

46. Androsace *septentrionalis,* L.—Hook. Fl. Bor. Am. ii. p. 119.

47. Primula *Hornemanniana,* Lehm.—Hook. Fl. Bor. Am. ii. p. 120.

POLYGONEÆ, *Juss.*

48. Polygonum *viviparum,* L.—Hook. Fl. Bor. Am. ii. p. 130.

AMENTACEÆ, *Juss.*

49. Salix *Richardsoni,* Hook. Fl. Bor. Am. ii. p. 147, Tab. 182.

50. Salix *vestita,* Ph.—Hook. Fl. Bor. Am. ii. p. 152.

51. Salix *Arctica,* Br.—Hook. Fl. Bor. Am. ii. p. 152.

52. Betula *glandulosa,* Mx.—Hook. Fl. Bor. Am. ii. p. 156.

53. Betula *nana,* L.—Hook. Fl. Bor. Am. ii. p. 156.

MONOCOTYLEDONES.

MELANTHACEÆ, *Br.*

54. Tofieldia *palustris*, Huds.—Hook. Fl. Bor. Am. ii.
p. 179.

ORCHIDEÆ, *Juss.*

55. Platanthera *obtusata*, Lindl.—Hook. Fl. Bor.
Am. ii. p. 196, Tab. 199.

56. Platanthera *rotundifolia*, Lindl.—Hook. Fl. Bor.
Am. ii. 200, Tab. 201.

CYPERACEÆ, *Juss.*

57. Carex *dioica*, L.—Hook. Fl. Bor. Am. ii. p. 208.

58. Carex *fuliginosa*, Sternb. and Hoppe.—Hook.
Fl. Bor. Am. ii. p. 224.

59. Eriophorum *capitatum*, Host,—Hook. Fl. Bor.
Am. ii. p. 231.

60. Eriophorum *polystachyon*, L.—Hook. Fl. Bor.
Am. ii. p. 231.

Collected between CHURCHILL *and* REPULSE BAY.

DICOTYLEDONES.

RANUNCULACEÆ, *Juss.*

1. Ranunculus *affinis*, Br. — Hook. Fl. Bor. Am.
i. p. 12, Tab. 6 A.

PAPAVERACEÆ, *Juss.*

2. Papaver *nudicaule*, L.—Hook. Fl. Bor. Am. i.
p. 34.

3. Arabis *petræa*, Lam.—Hook. Fl. Bor. Am. i. p. 42.

4. Cardamine *pratensis*, L.—Hook. Fl. Bor. Am. i.
p. 45.

5. Draba *alpina*, L.—Hook. Fl. Bor. Am. i. p. 50.

P

6. Eutrema *Edwardsii*, Br.—Hook. Fl. Bor. Am. i.
p. 67.

CARYOPHYLLEÆ, *Juss.*

7. Silene *acaulis*, L.—Hook. Fl. Bor. Am. i. p. 89.

8. Lychnis *apetala*, L.—Hook. Fl. Bor. Am. i. p. 94.

9. Stellaria *Edwardsii*, Br.—Hook. Fl. Bor. Am. i.
p. 96. Tab. 31.

10. Cerastium *alpinum*, L.—Hook. Fl. Bor. Am. i.
p. 104.

LEGUMINOSÆ, *Juss.*

11. Oxytropis *campestris*, De Cand.—Hook. Fl. Bor.
Am. i. p. 146.

12. Oxytropis *Uralensis*, De Cand.—Hook. Fl. Bor.
Am. i. p. 145.

13. Phaca *astragalina*, De Cand.—Hook. Fl. Bor.
Am. i. p. 145.

ROSACEÆ, *Juss.*

14. Dryas *integrifolia*, Vahl,—Hook. Fl. Bor. Am. i.
p. 174.

15. Rubus *Chamæmorus*, L.—Hook. Fl. Bor. Am. i.
p. 183.

16. Potentilla *nana*, Lehm.—Hook. Fl. Bor. Am. i.
p. 194.

ONAGRARIEÆ, *Juss.*

17. Epilobium *latifolium*, L.—Hook. Fl. Bor. Am. i.
p. 205.

SAXIFRAGEÆ, *Juss.*

18. Saxifraga *oppositifolia*, L.—Hook. Fl. Bor. Am. i.
p. 242.

19. Saxifraga *cæspitosa*, L.—Hook. Fl. Bor. Am. i.
p. 246.

20. Saxifraga *cernua*, L.—Hook. Fl. Bor. Am. i. p. 246.

21. Saxifraga *rivularis*, L.—Hook. Fl. Bor. Am. i.
p. 246.

211

22. Saxifraga *Hirculus*, L.—Hook. Fl. Bor. Am. i. p. 252. and var. *bi-triflora*.

23. Saxifraga *tricuspidata*, L.—Hook. Fl. Bor. Am. i. p. 253.

COMPOSITÆ, *Juss.*

24. Leontodon *Taraxacum*, L.—Hook, Fl. Bor. Am. i. p. 296.

25. Chrysanthemum *integrifolium*, Rich.—Hook. Fl. Bor. Am. i. p. 319, Tab. 109.

26. Erigeron *uniflorus*, L.—Hook. Fl. Bor. Am. ii. p. 17.

CAMPANULACEÆ, *Juss.*

27. Campanula *uniflora*, L.—Hook. Fl. Bor. Am. ii. p. 29.

ERICEÆ, *Juss.*

28. Andromeda *tetragona*, L.—Hook. Fl. Bor. Am. ii. p. 38.

29. Ledum *palustre*, L.—Hook. Fl. Bor. Am. ii. p. 44. var. *angustifolium*.

DIAPENSIACEÆ, *Lindl.*

30. Diapensia *Lapponica*, L.—Hook. Fl. Bor. Am. ii. p. 76.

BORAGINEÆ, *Juss.*

31. Lithospermum *maritimum*, Lehm.—Hook. Fl. Bor. Am. ii. p. 36.

SCROPHULARINEÆ, *Juss.*

32. Pedicularis *hirsuta*, L.—Hook. Fl. Bor. Am. ii. p. 109.

33. Pedicularis *Langsdorffii*, Fisch.—Hook. Fl. Bor. Am. ii. p. 109.

PLUMBAGINEÆ, *Juss.*

34. Statice *Armeria*, L.—Hook. Fl. Bor. Am. ii. p. 123.

AMENTACEÆ, *Juss.*

35. Salix *Myrsinites*, L.—Hook. Fl. Bor. Am. ii. p. 151.

36. Salix *Arctica*, Br.—Hook. Fl. Bor. Am. ii. p. 152.

MONOCOTYLEDONES.

JUNCEÆ, *Juss.*
37. Luzula *hyperborea,* Br.—Hook. Fl. Bor. Am. ii.
p. 188.
CYPERACEÆ, *Juss.*
38. Carex *membranacea,* Hook. Fl. Bor. Am. ii.
p. 220.
39. Eriophorum *polystachyon,* L.—Hook. Fl. Bor.
Am. ii. p. 231.
GRAMINEÆ, *Juss.*
40. Alopecurus *alpinus,* L.—Hook. Fl. Bor. Am. ii.
p. 234.
41. Hierochloe *alpina,* Rœm. et Sch.—Hook. Fl. Bor.
Am. ii. p. 234.
42. Colpodium *latifolium,* Br.— Hook. Fl. Bor.
Am. ii. p. 238.
43. Poa *Arctica,* Br.—Hook. Fl. Bor. Am. ii. p. 246.
44. Festuca *brevifolia,* Br.—Hook. Fl. Bor. Am. ii.
p. 250.
45. Elymus *arenarius,* L.—Hook. Fl. Bor. Am. ii.
p. 255.

Plants collected between REPULSE BAY *and* CAPE
LADY PELLY.

DICOTYLEDONES.

RANUNCULACEÆ, *Juss.*
1. Ranunculus *Lapponicus,* L.—Hook. Fl. Bor. Am.
i. p. 16.
PAPAVERACEÆ, *Juss.*
2. Papaver *nudicaule,* L.—Hook. Fl. Bor. Am. i.
p. 34.

CRUCIFERÆ, *Juss.*
 3. Cardamine *pratensis*, L.—Hook. Fl. Bor. Am. i.
  p. 44.
 4. Draba *alpina*, L.—Hook. Fl. Bor. Am. i. p. 50.
 5. Draba *stellata*, Jacq.—Hook. Fl. Bor. Am. i. p. 53.
CARYOPHYLLEÆ, *Juss.*
 6. Stellaria *humifusa*, Rottb.—Hook. Fl. Bor. Am. i.
  p. 97.
 7. Cerastium *alpinum*, L.—Hook. Fl. Bor. Am. i.
  p. 104.
LEGUMINOSÆ, *Juss.*
 8. Oxytropis *Uralensis*, De Cand.—Hook. Fl. Bor.
  Am. i. p. 145.
 9. Oxytropis *campestris*, De Cand.—Hook. Fl. Bor.
  Am. i. p. 147.
ROSACEÆ, *Juss.*
 10. Dryas *integrifolia*, Vahl,—Hook. Fl. Bor. Am. i.
  p. 174.
 11. Potentilla *nana*, Lehm.—Hook. Fl. Bor. Am. i.
  p. 190.
ONAGRARIEÆ, *Juss.*
 12. Epilobium *latifolium*, L.—Hook. Fl. Bor. Am. i.
  p. 204.
SAXIFRAGEÆ, *Juss.*
 13. Saxifraga *oppositifolia*, L.—Hook. Fl. Bor. Am. i.
  p. 242.
 14. Saxifraga *cernua*, L.—Hook. Fl. Bor. Am. i.
  p. 245.
 15. Saxifraga *rivularis*, L.—Hook. Fl. Bor. Am. i.
  p. 246.
 16. Saxifraga *nivalis*, L. — Hook. Fl. Bor. Am. i.
  p. 248.
 17. Saxifraga *foliolosa*, Br.—Hook. Fl. Bor. Am. i.
  p. 251.

18. Saxifraga *Hirculus,* L.—Hook. Fl. Bor. Am. i.
    p. 252.
COMPOSITÆ, *Juss.*
19. Leontodon *Taraxacum,* L. — Hook. Fl. Bor.
    Am. i. p. 296.
20. Pyrethrum *inodorum,* Sm.—Hook. Fl. Bor. Am. i.
    p. 320.
21. Arnica *montana,* L.— β. *angustifolia,* Hook, Fl.
    Bor. Am. i. p. 330.
22. Erigeron *uniflorus,* L.—Hook. Fl. Bor. Am. ii.
    p. 17.
ERICEÆ, *Juss.*
23. Andromeda *tetragona,* L.—Hook. Fl. Bor. Am. ii.
    p. 38.
MONOTROPEÆ, *Nutt.*
24. Pyrola *rotundifolia,* L.—Hook. Fl. Bor. Am. ii.
    p. 46.
SCROPHULARINEÆ, *Juss.*
25. Pedicularis *hirsuta,* L.—Hook. Fl. Bor. Am. ii.
    p. 109.
AMENTACEÆ, *Juss.*
26. Salix *Arctica,* Br.—Hook. Fl. Bor. Am. ii. p. 152.

MONOCOTYLEDONES.

JUNCEÆ, *Juss.*
27. Luzula *hyperborea,* Br.—Hook. Fl. Bor. Am. ii.
    p. 188.
CYPERACEÆ, *Juss.*
28. Carex *dioica,* L.—Hook. Fl. Bor. Am. ii. p. 208.
29. Carex *membranacea,* Hook. Fl. Bor. Am. ii.
    p. 220.
30. Carex *cæspitosa,* L. — Hook. Fl. Bor. Am. ii.
    p. 217.

31. Carex *ustulata,* Wahl.—Hook. Fl. Bor. Am. ii. p. 224.

32. Eriophorum *capitatum,* Host, — Hook. Fl. Bor. Am. ii. p. 231.

GRAMINEÆ, *Juss.*

33. Hierochloe *alpina,* Rœm. and Sch.—Hook. Fl. Bor. Am. ii. p. 234.

34. Colpodium *latifolium,* Br. — Hook. Fl. Bor. Am. ii. p. 238.

35. Dupontia *Fischeri,* Br.—Hook. Fl. Bor. Am. ii. p. 242.

36. Poa *Arctica,* Br.—Hook. Fl. Bor. Am. ii. p. 246.

37. Poa *angustata,* Br. — Hook. Fl. Bor. Am. ii. p. 246.

38. Poa *alpina,* L.—Hook. Fl. Bor. Am. ii. p. 246.

SPECIMENS OF ROCKS,

Described by JAMES TENNANT, ESQ., *Professor of Mineralogy in King's College, London.*

CAPE LADY PELLY, 67° 30′ N. 88° W.
Gneiss.

NEAR POINT HARGRAVE, 67° 25′ N. 87° 35′ W.
Gneiss.

CAPE T. SIMPSON, 67° 22′ N. 87° W.
Gneiss with chlorite.
Mica-slate.
Mica-slate, with indistinct crystals of precious Garnets.

ISTHMUS connecting Ross's Peninsula with the Continent.
Felspar.

SIMPSON'S PENINSULA, 68° ⅓ N. 88° 20′ W.

Compact argillaceous Limestone.

A HILL on the western shore of Halkett's Inlet, 69° 14′ N. 90° 50′ W.

Cellular Quartz, coloured by oxide of Iron.

Mica-slate full of Garnets.

HELEN ISLAND, one of the Harrison Group in Pelly Bay, 68° 54′ N. 89° 52′ W.

Felspar—red colour.

Gneiss; the Felspar, Mica, and Quartz distinctly stratified.

Gneiss; the Felspar red and greatly predominating.

BEACON HILL, near Fort Hope, 66° 32′ N. 86° 56′ W.

Granite.

Ditto, with a small quantity of Mica; the Felspar red, and constituting four-fifths of the mass.

Gneiss, with veins of red Felspar running diagonally to the stratification.

Mica-slate.

NORTH POLE RIVER.

Mica-slate.

Ditto, with veins of Quartz.

Gneiss.

Ditto, the Felspar red and greatly predominating.

Ditto, the Felspar very friable.

Quartz rock with Felspar.

Argillaceous Limestone, compact.

NORTH POLE LAKE, 66° 40′ N. 87° 2′ W.

Gneiss.

Mica-slate.

REPULSE BAY, 66° 32 N. 86° 56′ W.

Quartz, coloured by oxide of Iron, and containing minute particles of Gold.

MELVILLE PENINSULA, 68° 27′ N. 85° 24′ W.

Hornblende-slate.

MUNRO INLET.

Granite, the Felspar greatly predominating.

ISLAND near the north point of Rankin's Inlet.

Quartz, enclosing chlorite and Copper Pyrites.

Talcose-slate.

Carbonate and silicate of Copper, with Copper Pyrites on argillaceous slate.

Ditto, with a thin coating of green carbonate of Copper.

Mica-slate.

Chlorite-slate, friable.

Ditto, with very thin veins of Calcareous Spar running diagonally in stratification.

ISLAND near the south point of Rankin's Inlet.

Quartz and Iron Pyrites; the latter crystallized in cubes, the faces of which are not above one-sixteenth of an inch.

Quartz, with Iron Pyrites, and superficially coloured by oxide of Iron.

Hornblende-slate.

Mica-slate.

Chlorite-slate.

Dip of the needle and force of magnetic attraction at various stations along the west shore of Hudson's Bay, and at Fort Hope, Repulse Bay.

Name of Station.	Latitude N.			Longitude W.			Date.	Times.		Dip Mean.			Time of 10 Vibrations.	Therm.			Variation of Compass.		
	deg.	mi.	sec.	deg.	mi.	sec.		h.	mi.	deg.	mi.	sec.	Needle No. 2 deflected, 30 deg. from dip.	deg.	mi.	sec.	deg.	mi.	sec.
York Factory	57	0	2	92	26	0	5 Nov. 1845	9	0 A.M.	83	47	0		+31	0				
„	57	0	0	92	26	0	8 „	9	0 „	83	43	0		+25	0				
„		„			„		12 „	2	30 P.M.	83	37	0		+25	0				
„		„			„		15 „	9	0 A.M.	83	41	0		+33	0				
„	57	0	0	92	26	0	19 „	9	0 „	83	42	5		+25	0				
„		„			„		22 „	9	30 „	83	43	4		+ 3	0				
„		„			„		26 „	9	30 „	83	48	7		— 4	0				
„		„			„		29 „	9	30 „	83	42	5		—13	0				
„		„			„		3 Dec. „	9	30 „	83	54	2		— 6	0				
„		„			„		6 „	9	30 „	83	43	2		+ 8	0				
„		„			„		10 „	9	30 „	83	43	5		—19	0				
„		„			„		13 „	9	30 „	83	48	2		0	0				

Name of Station.	Latitude N.	Longitude W.	Date.	Times.	Dip Mean.	Time of 10 Vibrations. Needle No. 2 deflected, 20 deg. from dip.	Therm.	Variation of Compass.
	deg. mi. sec.	deg. mi. sec.		h. mi.	deg. mi. sec.		deg. mi.	deg. mi. sec.
York Factory	57 0 0	92 26 0	17 Dec. 1845	9 35 A.M.	83 40 9		−11 0	
"	"	"	20 "	9 30 "	83 39 1		−16 0	
"	"	"	24 "	10 10 "	83 45 5		−23 0	
"	"	"	31 "	10 30 "	83 46 0		+ 7 0	
"	"	"	3 Jan. 1846	10 30 "	83 46 1		+20 0	
"	"	"	7 "	10 30 "	83 47 0		+ 5 0	
"	"	"	10 "	10 30 "	83 45 5		+ 7 0	
"	"	"	14 "	10 30 "	83 43 9		− 2 0	
"	"	"	21 "	10 30 "	83 44 8		−10 0	
"	"	"	24 "	10 30 "	83 41 7		+23 5	
"	"	"	28 "	10 30 "	83 45 8		+15 0	
"	"	"	31 "	10 0 A.M. / 3 0 P.M.	83 45 8		−15 5 / −3 0	
"	"	"	4 Feb. "	10 0 A.M. / 3 0 P.M.	83 50 5		−12 5 / −14 0	
"	"	"	7 "	10 0 A.M.	83 45 5		−11 5	

Name of Station.	Latitude N. deg. mi. sec.	Longitude W. deg. mi. sec.	Date.	Times. h. mi.	Dip Mean. deg. mi. sec.	Time of 10 Vibrations. Needle No. 2 deflected, 20 deg. from dip.	Therm. deg. mi.	Variation of Compass. deg. mi. sec.
York Factory......	57 0 0	92 26 0	11 Feb. 1846	10 0 A.M.	83 44 8	}	− 5 0	
"	"	"		3 30 P.M.	83 41 6		−11 3	
"	"	"	14 "	9 30 A.M.	83 38 1		−23 0	
"	"	"		3 20 P.M.	83 36 6		− 8 0	
"	"	"	18 "	9 30 A.M.	88 41 0		+ 6 0	
"	"	"		3 30 P.M.			− 3 5	
"	"	"	21 "	9 30 A.M.	88 40 9		−11 0	
"	"	"		3 30 P.M.			+ 6 0	
"	"	"	25 "	9 30 A.M.	88 39 7		−23 5	
"	"	"		3 30 P.M.			−10 5	
"	"	"	28 "	9 30 A.M.	83 44 1		−13 0	
"	"	"		3 30 P.M.			+ 4 5	
"	"	"	4 Mar. "	9 30 A.M.	83 42 5		+ 6 0	
"	"	"		3 30 P.M.			+ 4 5	
"	"	"	7 "	9 30 A.M.	88 44 6		+29 0	
"	"	"		3 40 P.M.			+37 0	
"	"	"	11 "	9 30 A.M.	88 40 9		+26 0	
"	"	"		3 30 P.M.			+25 5	
"	"	"	14 "	9 30 A.M.	88 40 6		+12 0	
"	"	"		3 30 P.M.			+22 5	
"	"	"	18 "	9 30 A.M.	88 39 6		+15 0	
"	"	"		3 40 P.M.			+21 5	
"	"	"	21 "	9 30 A.M.	88 37 7		− 2 5	
"	"	"		3 30 P.M.			+ 5 8	
"	"	"	25 "	9 40 A.M.	88 47 0		+30 0	
"	"	"		3 30 P.M.			+30 0	
"	"	"	28 "	9 35 A.M.	83 43 8		+ 8 0	
"	"	"		3 30 P.M.			+ 8 0	

Name of Station.	Latitude N. (deg. mi. sec.)	Longitude W. (deg. mi. sec.)	Date.	Times. (h. mi.)	Dip Mean. (deg. mi. sec.)	Time of 10 Vibrations. (Needle No. 2 deflected, 20 deg. from dip.)	Therm. (deg. mi.)	Variation of Compass. (deg. mi. sec.)
York Factory......	57 0 0	92 26 0	1 April 1846	9 30 A.M.	83 42 8		+8 0	
				3 30 P.M.			+15 0	
„		„	4 „	9 30 A.M.	83 45 2		+35 0	
				3 30 P.M.			+25 0	
„		„	11 „	9 40 A.M.	83 40 6		+41 0	
				3 30 P.M.			+42 0	
„		„	15 „	9 35 A.M.	83 35 7		—3 5	
				3 30 P.M.			—6 0	
„		„	18 „	9 30 A.M.	83 40 2		+9 0	
				3 30 P.M.			+29 0	
„		„	22 „	10 30 A.M.	83 38 9		+45 0	
				3 35 P.M.			+40 0	
„		„	25 „	10 0 A.M.	83 35 5	Ther. +41° 0' 21s.-34	+43 0	
				3 30 P.M.			+32 0	
„		„	29 „	9 45 A.M.	83 38 0	Ther. +46° 0' 21s.-23	+42 0	
				3 30 P.M.			+43 0	
„		„	2 May „	9 30 A.M.	83 38 5		+39 0	
				3 30 P M.			+47 0	
„		„	6 „	9 30 A.M.	83 37 9	Ther. +66° 0' 21s.-31	+51 0	
				3 30 P.M.			+67 0	
„		„	16 „	9 35 A.M.	83 39 0	Ther. +43° 0' 21s.-13	+36 0	
				3 35 P.M.			+44 0	
Creek..........	58 2 0	92 20 0	20 June „	3 45 P.M.	84 46 4		+49 0	
Churchill	58 43 50	94 14 0	29 „	9 47 A.M.	84 50 8	Ther. +61° 0' 21s.-14	+60 0	
				3 35 P.M.			+61 0	
„	„	„	1 July „	10 30 A.M.	84 43 9		+88 0	
				3 0 P.M.			+60 0	

Name of Station.	Latitude N.			Longitude W.			Date.	Times.		Dip Mean.				Time of 10 Vibrations.	Therm.			Variation of Compass.		
	deg.	mi.	sec.	deg.	mi.	sec.		h.	mi.	deg.	mi.	sec.		Needle No. 2 deflected, 20 deg. from dip.	deg.	mi.	sec.	deg.	mi.	sec.
Churchill	58	43	50	94	14	0	4 July 1846	8	10 P.M.	84	44	5			+41	0				
Knapp's Bay......	61	9	42	,,			8 ,,	10	45 A.M.	86	18	3			+52	0				
,,	,,			,,			8 ,,	3	0 P.M.						+51	0				
,,	,,			,,			12 ,,	5	15 P.M.	87	16	3			+58	0				
,,	64	6	0	88	0	0	18 ,,	Noon.		86	36	5		Ther.+54° 0' 20s.-84	+52	0				
Near Wager River	65	10	0	,,			21 ,,	4	5 P.M.	87	10	6		Ther.+65° 5' 21s.-03	+54	0				
,,	65	15	36	87	10	0	22 ,,	11	35 A.M.						+52	0				
Repulse Bay......	66	32	0	,,			27 ,,	11	15 A.M.	88	16	7		Ther.+57° 5' 21s.-7	+52	0				
Flett's Portage				,,			28 ,,	2	40 P.M						+55	0				
								3	15 P.M.						+57	0				
Descent Portage ..				,,			31 ;,,	6	20 P.M.						+90	0				
								6	50 P.M.						+82	0				
Cape Lady Pelly ..	,,			,,			3 Aug. ,,								+53	0				
3 Miles N.W. of do.	,,			,,			,,	5	30 P.M.	88	27	1		Ther.+52° 0' 21s.-8	+52	0				
Fort Hope	66	32	0	86	56	0	18 Nov. ,,	11	15 A.M.	87	51	5			— 6	0		*West*		
								2	0 P.M.						— 5	0		62	50	30
,,				,,			21 ,,	9	45 A.M.	88	11	4		Ther.+10° 5' 22s.-66	+ 6	0				
								2	15 P.M.						+10	0				

Name of Station.	Latitude N.			Longitude W.			Date.	Times.		Dip Mean.			Time of 10 Vibrations.	Therm.		Variation of Compass.		
	deg.	mi.	sec.	deg.	mi.	sec.		h.	mi.	deg.	mi.	sec.		deg.	mi.	deg.	mi.	sec.
Fort Hope	66	32	0	86	56	0	25 Nov. 1846	2	10 P.M.	88	8	9	*Needle No. 2 deflected, 20 deg. from dip.*	—21	0			
,,	,,			,,			5 Dec. ,,	10	0 A.M.	88	13	9	*Ther.* + 9° 0'	—15	0			
								2	0 P.M.				22s·6	—13	0			
,,	,,			,,			12 ,,	10	10 A.M.	88	13	3		—16	0			
								2	5 P.M.					+6	0			
,,	,,			,,			16 ,,	10	0 A.M.	88	12	7		+8	0			
								2	20 P.M.					+ 0	0			
,,	,,			,,			23 ,,	10	0 A.M.	88	16	3		+2	0			
								2	0 P.M.					+7	0			
,,	,,			,,			2 Jan. 1847	10	10 A.M.	88	17	5		—8	0			
								2	30 P.M.					—23	0			
,,	,,			,,			10 Feb. ,,	9	50 A.M.	88	10	9		—21	0			
								2	10 P.M.					—22	0			
,,	,,			,,			13 ,,	9	50 A.M.	88	13	5		—20	0			
								2	10 P.M.					—28	0			
,,	,,			,,			17 ,,	9	50 A.M.					—26	0			
								2	15 P.M.					—36	0			
,,	,,			,,			24 ,,	9	55 A.M.					—33	0			
								2	10 P.M.					—22	0			
York Factory......	57	0	0	92	26	0	18 Sept. ,,	9	15 A.M.	83	47	0		—22	0			
								3	10 P.M.					+52	0			

FORT HOPE, REPULSE BAY.—*Abstract of*

Day of the Month.	Temperature of the Atmosphere taken eight times in twenty-four hours.			Prevailing Winds.	
	Highest.	Lowest.	Mean.	Direction.	Force.
	deg.m.	deg.m.			
1	+35	+27	+29.7	E.S.E	2—4
2	+37	+27	+31	E.S.E.	5—4
3	+36	+25	+31	E.—Vble.	9—1
4	+34	+28	+30.3	E. by S.	8
5	+42	+26	+32.7	O.—N.N.W.	0—7
6				N.	6
7	+31	+25	+27	N.	6
8	+35	+26	+30.5	N.N.W.	6
9				N.N.W.	6
10	+32	+30	+31.3	N.N.W.—O.—S.E.	4—5
11	+34	+31	+32.5	E. by S.	10—8
12				E. by S.—S. E. by E.	9—5
13				S.W. by S.—S.W.	5—9
14					
15	+45	+45	+45	S.S.E.	4
16	+34	+25	+28.7	Vble.—O.—E. by N.	1—2
17	+32	+24	+28	W.	2—3
18	+29	+26	+27.7	N.W.—W.N.W.	6—7
19	+33	+26	+29.7	W.N.W.—O.—E.	9—0
20	+32	+24	+28	N.N.W.	5—4
21	+36	+24	+29.3	N.—O.—E.	0 3
22	+31	+23	+27.7	N. by W.	5—6
23	+28	+16	+22.3	W.N.W.	3—4
24	+42	+21	+29.3	Vble.	1—0
25	+30	+16	+24.3	Vble.	0—2
26	+30	+26	+28	E.N.E.	8—9
27	+26	+24	+25	N. by W.	5—6
28	+26	+20	+22.7	N.N.W.	7—6
29	+24	+22	+23	W.N.W.	4
30	+22	+18	+19.7	Vble.—S.E. by E.	1—4
			714.4		
			+28.57		

Meteorological Journal for September, 1846.

| Barometer and Thermometer attached. | | Remarks on the Weather, &c. |
Barom.	Thermo.	
....	....	c. c. o. Solar halo with parhelia.
....	....	c. c. c.
....	....	s. b. c.
....	....	c. c. c. p. of sleet.
....	....	c. c. o. Full moon.
....	....	p. s. o.
....	....	p. s. c.
....	....	c. p. s.
....	....	c. p. s.
....	....	c. b. c. o.
....	....	s. c. s. c. b. much drift.
....	....	o. c. c. ☾ last quarter.
....	....	b. c.
....	....	c. p. s.
....	....	c. c. c.
....	....	b. c.
....	....	o. s. s.
....	....	s. s.
....	....	s. o. c s.
....	....	c. c. c.
....	....	s. s. b. Aurora visible to the southward at 8 p m.
....	....	b. b. c.
....	....	o. b. c. o.
....	....	c. o.
....	....	s. s. s.
....	....	s. drifting.
....	....	p. so. drifting.
....	....	b. c.
....	....	h. b. s.

P

FORT HOPE, REPULSE BAY.—*Abstract of*

Day of the Month.	Temperature of the Atmosphere taken eight times in twenty-four hours.			Prevailing Winds.	
	Highest.	Lowest.	Mean.	Direction.	Force.
	deg.m.	deg.m.	deg.m.		
1	+27	+25.	+26	Vble S.W.—N.W.	1—5
2	+25	+16	+21	N.W.	8
3	+24	+10	+18	Vble. E. by S.	1—5
4	+38	+38	+38	S.E. by E.	4
5	+37	+30	+33	E.	2—4
6	+33	+28	+30.3	N.E.	3—4
7	+30	+28	+29	N.E.	4—3
8	+28	+25	+26.3	N.—N.N.W.	4—5
9	+22	+21	+21.5	N.W.—O.—Vble.	3—0—2
10	+27	+26	+26.5	E.	8—9
11	+32	+28	+30	N.E.—O.	1—0
12	+27	+25	+25	N. by W.	7—9
13	+29	+27	+28.1	N. by W.	8—9
14	+26	+18	+23.2	N.	10—11
15	+12	+10	+11	N. by W.	10—11
16	+ 5	0	+ 2.6	N.N.W.	7—4
17	+ 3.5	— 1	+ 0.8	N.N.W.	7—8
18	+ 6	— 0.8	+ 1.7	S.W.W.—W.N.W.	4—6
19	+ 2	— 4.8	— 0.7	N.—N.N.W.	5—9
20	+ 3	— 2.5	— 0.3	N.W.	10—11
21	— 2.8	—10	— 6	N W.—N.W.byN.	7—11
22	— 4.5	—15	— 8.1	N.W. Vble. S.W.	0—2
23	+ 5.3	— 0.5	+ 3	N.W. by W.—N.W. by N.	3—5
24	— 0.	— 6.4	— 4.2	N.W.byW—N.W.	4—5
25	+ 4.5	— 6.2	— 1.8	N.W. by N.	5
26	— 7.3	—10.2	— 8.5	N.W.—N.W.by N.	4—6
27	— 6.	—15	—10.6	N.W.by N.—N.W.	0—3—5
28	— 1.8	—11.8	— 6.4	N.W. & N.N.W.	0—4
29	+10	+ 3.1	+ 8.4	S.S.E. S.—calm.	0—2—4
30	+25.3	+21	+23.4	S.S.E.—S.W.—W. by N.	2—8
31	+10	0	+ 5.2	S. N.W. W.S.W. N.N.W.	1—4
			389.4		
			+12.56		

Meteorological Journal for October, 1846.

Barometer and Thermometer attached.		Remarks on the Weather, &c.
Barom.	*Thermo.*	
....	....	s. ps.
....	....	b. c. drifting.
....	....	h. p. s. o. s.
....	....	h. p. r.
....	....	h. wet.
....	....	h. p. s. o. p. s.
....	....	h. p. s.
....	....	c. o. o.
....	....	h. c. c.
....	....	s. drifting.
....	....	s. s. s.
....	...	s. with much drift.
29.338	+49	s. and much drift.
29.431	+46.3	s. and drift.
29.690	+44	s. much drift.
29.605	+30.5	b. c. ; drift; haze and some drift—parhelia; haze with scaly snow; faint aurora to the S. and S. by E. alt. 12°.
29.719	+32.8	b. c., much drift ; aurora to the S.S.E. parallel to the horizon ; alt. 12°.
29.641	+31.5	b. c., drift; cirrus ; some faint streaks of aurora to the W.
29.662	+29	b. c., drifting ; solar halo with prismatic colours and parhelia; snow and much drift.
29.842	+29.5	s. much drift.
29.959	+30.5	b. c., much drift ; at 8 P.M. several streaks of faint aurora extending across the zenith in a N.W. and S.E. direction ; many rays in different parts of the heavens.
29.828	+28.5	.
29.919	+32	f. o. f. o. s. o. s. b. c. f. s.
29.974	+31	b. c. o. drifting.
30.023	+29	o. drifting.
30.062	+29.3	o. m. b. c. drifting.
30.47	+26.5	b. c. m., some faint streaks of aurora in various parts of the sky bearing for the most part N.N.W. and S.S.E.
30.505	+26.	b. c., a few clouds near horizon ; a very faint light yellow cloud aurora to the S.E. and N.W.
30.119	+30.3	c. s. b. c. s. o. m. b. c., cirrus extending from S.S.E. to N.N.W., resembling much the aurora. Lunar halo.
29.078	+39.7	o. m. o. s. b. c. o. drifting.
30.094	+34.3	b. b. c. c., solar halo ; cirrus ; 120 lunar distances were observed from Jupiter and at. Aquilæ, E. and W. of the moon. Lunar halo diam. 40° or 50°.

FORT HOPE, REPULSE BAY.—*Abstract of*

Day of the Month.	Temperature of the Atmosphere taken eight times in twenty-four hours.			Prevailing Winds.	
	Highest.	Lowest.	Mean.	Direction.	Force.
	deg.m.	deg.m.	deg.m.		
1	+18	— 3.0	+ 8.5	W.N.W. N.E. E.	2—7
2	+26.5	+22.3	+24.4	S.E. S.E. by E. E. by W.	2—5
3	+27	+25.5	+26.3	S.E. E.S.E.	2—5
4	+26	+21.5	+23.8	S.E.S. S.S.E.	3—5
5	+22	+ 0	+13.2	N. by W. N.W. by W.	2—7
6	— .5	— 9.5	— 3.5	W.N.W.	3—7
7	+11.5	+ 6	+ 9.7	N. by E.	4—7
8	+11	+ 5	+ 8.5	N.	4—7
9	+12.5	+ 9 5	+10.9	E.N.E. N.E.	3—10
10	+28.2	+22.5	+25.6	E.S.E. S. S.S.W.	3—8
11	+17	+ 2.5	+ 7.5	N.W. N.N.W. W. by N.	5—8
12	+ 2.3	— 8.5	— 1	N.N.E. W. N.N.W.	2—5
13	— 6	— 8	— 6.8	N. by W. N.N.W.	4—8
14	— 4.6	— 8.7	— 6.6	N.N.W. N. N. by W.	3—7
15	+ 4.5	—10.5	— 3.8	Calm. Vble. E.	0—4
16	+17.3	+15	+16.3	E. N.E. N.	1—6
17	+ 7.5	— 8	+ .25	N. by W.	4—6
18	— 4	— 9.2	— 7.1	N.W. by N. Calm S.W.	0-2
19	+21.7	+18	+20.61	S.S.E. S.E. E.	4—7
20	+12	— 8.8	+ 2.9	Calm. S. by E. N.	0—2
21	+ 4.5	— 4.2	— 0.9	S. S.E. E.	4—1
22	— 3	— 4.2	— 3.6	S. by E. W. N.W.	2—6
23	—18.5	—22.5	—19.77	N. by W. N.N.W.	3—5
24	—20.5	—25.2	—22.54	N.N.W.	5—1
25	—14.5	—24.5	—20.06	N.by E. N.W. N.W.by W.	1—3
26	—17.5	—23.5	—20.7	N.	6—9
27	—11.8	—15.5	—13.6	N. by W.	9—10
28	— 5.4	— 8.5	— 6.6	N. by W.	7—9
29	—16.5	—25.3	—20.3	N.N.W. W.N.W.	6—3
30	—17.5	—24.4	—21.	W. W.N.W. N.W.	6—3
			+20.59		
			+ 0.68		

Meteorological Journal for November, 1846.

Barometer and Thermometer attached.		Remarks on the Weather, &c.
Barom.	*Thermo.*	
30.011	+35	b. c. o. s. and drift.
29.715	+38	o. m s. o m. o s.
29.623	+38.7	o. m s. o s.
29.624	+39.5	o. m. b c. o m.
29.796	+41	o. m s. b c. b. drifting. A faint ray of aurora to the S. E. extending vertically towards the zenith.
30.009	+38.8	b. c. drifting. Some faint beams of aurora extending from S.W. to N.W., alt. 60°, one ray to the S.E. pointing towards the zenith.
29.894	+37.3	o. c. o. drifting.
30.1	+39.5	o. drifting.
39.996	+35.2	o. s. drifting thick.
29.598	+40.2	o s. o. b. c. o. much drift.
29.728	+38	o. s. o. m. b. c. drifting.
30.163	+38.1	b. c. m. b. drifting.
30.214	+34.9	b. m. b c. m. much drift.
30.39	+36.2	b. m. much drift. Solar halo and parhelia with prismatic colours; hazy near horizon; a faint beam of aurora to the westward directed toward the zenith; drifting.
30.239	+37	o. m. o. s.
29.963	+38	o. s. b. c. m. drifting.
30.102	+37	o. s. b. c. m. drifting. Three beams of aurora pointing towards the zenith; two of them bearing N.N.W., and the other S.E.
30.006	+33.7	b. c. fo. o. m. At 9 A.M. there was a very red sky to the N. westward; sound heard at a great distance.
29.573	+36.7	o. s. b. c. drifting.
29.420	+36.8	o. s. m. o. s. f. b. c. m. At 7 h. 30 m. a faint aurora extending from W. to S.E., alt. 20°; motion rapid; no prismatic colours.
29.409	+37	o. s. b. c. s. o. f. s. b. m. s.
29.615	+39	b. c. Some faint streaks of aurora, most of them to the S. eastward, and pointed towards the zenith.
29.918	+33.7	b. m. b. c. Some faint rays of aurora visible this morning at 5 h. 30 m. in different parts of the heavens; drifting.
30.408	+33.7	b. c. drifting.
30.573	+30.8	b. b. m. Two faint beams of aurora bearing W.N.W. and pointing towards the zenith; altitude of lower limb 30°.
30.606	+32	b. m. b. much drift.
29.555	+31	b. m. o. s. drifting. Door drifted up.
29.41	+26.6	o. m. b. c. s. o. s. drifting.
29.894	+27.5	b. c. drifting.
30.354	+26	b. c. m. drifting.

FORT HOPE, REPULSE BAY.—*Abstract of*

Day of the Month.	Temperature of the Atmosphere taken eight times in twenty-four hours.			Prevailing Winds.	
	Highest.	Lowest.	Mean.	Direction.	Force.
	deg.m.	*deg.m.*	*deg.m.*		
1	—24	—27	—25.875	Calm. N.E. N.	0—3
2	—26.7	—30	—28.1	N.E. Calm. N.	1—0
3	—24.8	—28.5	—26.4	N. by W.	1—4
4	—24.8	—28	—29.97	N.W. by W. S.S.W.	4—0
5	—17.3	—21	—19.7	Calm. S. by E. S.S.E.	0—2
6	— 6.5	—11	— 9.14	E. by S. N.E. N.	5—2
7	—16.5	—24	—19.7	N.	5—7
8	—19.5	—25.6	—22.61	N.	9—8
9	+14	—15	+ .03	N.N.W. N.N.E. N.E.	11—5
10	+17	+14.8	+15.74	N.E. by N. N.E. E.	4—6
11	+12.7	+ 9.8	+11.6	N. by E. N.N.W. N.W.	4—1
12	+ 4	— 6	+ .74	S. S.S.E. Calm.	0—3
13	—13	—17	—14.93	N. N. by W.	4—1
14	—19	—23	—20.94	Calm. Vble.	0—2
15	— 9	—19	—16.55	N.N.W. N. by W.	1—4
16	0	— 3	— 1.64	N. E.N.E. Calm. Vble.	0—1
17	— 5	— 9.6	— 6.05	Vble. W.N.W.	1—2
18	— 6	— 8.5	— 7.04	N. by W. W. Vble.	2—1
19	—14.2	—20	—17.4	N. by W. N.N.W.	5—4
20	— 8.7	—13	—10.56	S. by W. N. by W. N.	1—4
21	—20.7	—32.3	—24.83	N.W. Vble. N.	1—2
22	—30.5	—36.5	—33.4	W. Calm. N. by E.	0—2
23	—21.4	—26	—23.3	N.N.E. N.E.N.	0—1
24	—31	—35.3	—33.13	N.	7—10
25	—36	—38	—36.83	N. by W.	10—8
26	—34	—38	—36.46	N. by W. N.	8—11
27	—30	—30	—30	N.	10—11
28	—30.8	— 34.8	—33.01	N. N. by W.	6—4
29	—24.5	—40	—35	N.W. by W. Vble. N.N.W.	0—5
30	—25	—32.3	—29.63	N.	6—9
31	—23	—32.5	—29.25	N. by W. Vble. N.	1—7
			597.43		
			—19.27		

Meteorological Journal for December, 1846.

Barometer and Thermometer attached.		Remarks on the Weather, &c.
Barom.	Thermo.	
30.452	+18.75	b. c.
30.237	+19.6	b. c. b. c. m. Lunar halo.
30.886	+16.3	b. c. b. c. m.
30.013	+17	b. c. m.
29.778	+17.6	b. c. m. parhelia with prismatic colours; aurora visible to the south in two arches arising from near the horizon to the zenith.
29.480	+27.5	o. s. b. c.
29.764	+26	b. m. c. drifting.
30.039	+23	b. c. drift.
29.974	+22	s. o. drifting.
29.892	+28.3	s. o. b. c. o. s. drifting.
29.759	+32	o. s. m.
30.016	+26.6	o. m. s. b. m.
30.36	+31	b. m. b. c. The sky to the north had a beautiful lake coloured tint at sunset; the most brilliant display of aurora I have observed this winter, the centre being towards the true south, and gradually rising from an altitude of 12° to 70° or 80°. It was of a pale yellowish green colour. Horizontal needle not affected.
30.473	+26	b. c. m. Some faint beams of aurora in different parts of the heavens. A very faint aurora to the southward.
30.37	+27	b. m. b. c. o. A very faint aurora; centre true south.
30.186	+30.7	o. m.
30.205	+27.6	o. m. b. m. Wind variable from N. to E.; faint aurora to the S.; alt. 10°; centre S.S.W. 30°.
30.274	+29.3	o. b. c. m. Aurora faint to the S. by W.
30.245	+27.3	b. c. m. drifting.
30.259	+28	b. c. o. s.
30.268	+29	b. m. Arch of aurora across zenith nearly east and west; brightest at western extremity.
30.264	+22.3	b. c. b. m.
30.168	+25.3	b. m. b. c. b. m. s. Speculæ of snow falling. Lunar halo faint.
30.065	+23.6	b. m. much drift.
29.996	+22	b. m. much drift.
29.83	+20	b. c. m. much drift.
29.523	+15.5	b. c. m. much drift.
29.536	+14.3	b. m. b. drifting.
29.603	+14.3	b. b. c. A faint halo, centre S., alt. about 20°; wind variable from N. to W. by S.; cirrus clouds; halo round moon.
29.577	+11.6	b. c. drifting; much drift.
29.564	+15.3	b. c.

FORT HOPE, REPULSE BAY.—*Abstract of*

Day of the Month.	Temperature of the Atmosphere taken eight times in twenty-four hours.			Prevailing Winds.	
	Highest.	Lowest.	Mean.	Direction.	Force.
	deg.m.	deg.m.	deg.m.		
1	—23.5	—32	—26.96	N.N.W. N.W.byW. N.byW.	1—6
2	—29.5	—33.5	—31.8	N.N.W. N. by W. N.W.	2—5
3	—30.3	—32	—31.4	N. by W. Calm. N.N.E.	0—1
4	—31	—34	—32.82	N. Calm. N.	0—2
5	—27.5	—30	—28.61	N. ½ W.	5—8
6	—26.5	—31	—28.3	N.N.W.	6—8
7	—40	—42	—40.9	N.W. Calm. W. N.W.N.	0—1
8	—44	—47	—46.7	N.W. N.N.W. N. by W.	1—7
9	—38	—40	—39	N.	10—11
10	—12	—17	—14.5	N.N.W.	10—12
11	—10	—10	—10	N. by W.	7—11
12	—12	—16	—14	N. by W.	7—8
13	—28.5	—33.5	—30.8	N.N.W. N. by W.	6—7
14	—33.8	—36.3	—35.1	N.byW. N.½W. N.by W.	7—5
15	—38	—39.5	—38.7	N.by W. N.W. N.N.W.	2—5
16	—39.3	—41	—37.07	N. by W. N.N.W. N.byW.	2—6
17	—38	—41	—39.6	N. by W.	7—8
18	—37	—40	—38.95	N.W. by N. N.by W.	2—4
19	—25	—31	—30.6	N.N.W. N.N.W.	9—11
20	—14	—20	—17	N.N.W.	8—10
21	—20.5	—26.5	—23.4	N. by W. N.N.E. N.	2—9
22	—14	—26	—18.87	N.W. N.N.W.	6—11
23	—10	—13	—11.2	N.N.W.	9—11
24	—13	—13	—13	N.N.W.	9—11
25	—26.5	—32.5	—29.25	N.N.W.	4—7
26	—31.5	—37	—34.47	N. Calm. Vble. N.	0—1
27	—29	—35	—32.05	N. N. by W.	1—2
28	—33.3	—35.5	—34.65	N. by W.	6—7
29	—36	—42.7	—39.25	N. by W. W.N.W. N.W.	4—1
30	—24.7	—36.5	—28.64	S. by W. Vble. E.	1—5
31	—27.5	—35	—31.5	N. by W.	4—7
			909		
			—29.32		

Meteorological Journal for January, 1847.

Barometer and Thermometer attached.		Remarks on the Weather, &c.
Barom.	*Thermo.*	
29.908	+17.	b. c. b. c. s. drifting.
30.128	+16	b. m. b. Faint aurora, centre S.W. by S., alt. 15°; drifting; some streaks of aurora to the southward pointing to the zenith.
30.134	+18.5	b. c. b. Much refraction; thermometer in house +11°; a beam of aurora to the south pointing to the zenith.
30.023	+15.6	b. b. Hills much refracted; aurora faint; centre of arch S. by W.; alt. 10°; aurora in a narrow line parallel to horizon, alt. 4°, extent 70°, centre south.
29.93	+14.6	b. c. m. drifting.
30.04	+14.6	b. m. drifting. A faint aurora extending from S.S.E. across the zenith.
29.861	+12.6	b. c. m. Mercury froze after two hours' exposure.
29.8	+11	b. b. drifting.
29.974	....	Much drift; could not get out to see thermometer, door being drifted up.
29.139	+ 6	o. o. Much drift; obliged to take the thermometers into the house, as the pillars of snow on which the posts were placed were nearly all blown away.
29.193	+10.5	o. b. m. Much drift; a beam of aurora S.E.; alt. 25°.
29.309	+14.5	b. m. Much drift; very faint aurora; centre W. by N.; alt. 10°.
29.549	+12.3	b. m. drifting; a very faint aurora, centre S.S.W., alt. 16°; extent 60° or 70°.
29.588	+13	b. c. m. drift; arch of aurora faint, alt. 11°, centre S.S.W., extent 90°.
29.608	+ 7.6	b. m. c. Streams of bright light shooting from the sun to the alt. of 5°.
29.67	+ 7	b. c. b. drifting, stratus; arch of aurora faint, centre south, alt. 18°, extent 60°. Centre S.S.W., alt. 12°, extent 90°.
29.887	+13	b. m. drifting. Aurora visible, faint but brightest to the westward; centre S., alt. 60°.
29.245	+ 6	b. c. b. c. m. A very faint arch of aurora from N.W. by N. extending across zenith.
29.662	+ 7	m. o. much drift; door drifted up.
29.472	+11	o. q. much drift.
29.604	+ 9.5	b. m. much drift.
29.445	+ 8	b. m. o s. o. m. q. s. o. q. drifting.
29.273	+ 9.5	o. m. much drift.
29.366	+10	o q. gale all night; much drift.
29.83	+ 8	b. m. drifting; solar halo with parhelia.
30.035	+ 6.3	b. A faint arch of aurora across zenith S.W. and N.E.
29.911	+ 4.6	b. c. b. c. s. o. m. o. s.
29.908	+ 7.3	b. m. drifting. Very cold to the sensation; spiculæ of snow falling; a broad band of aurora, the lower edge having a reddish or lake tint, running parallel to the horizon, alt. 2°, centre S.W., extent 70°; some beams of aurora S.E. pointing towards the zenith.
29.954	+ 7.3	b. m.
29.737	+ 5.6	o. b. c. m. s. b. c. s.
29.714	+ 8	b. c. m. Cirrus; drifting.

FORT HOPE, REPULSE BAY.—*Abstract of*

Day of the Month.	Temperature of the Atmosphere taken eight times in twenty-four hours.			Prevailing Winds.	
	Highest.	Lowest.	Mean.	Direction.	Force.
	deg.m.	deg.m.	deg.m.		
1	—29.8	—38.5	—33.65	N.N.W. N.W. W.	6—1
2	—30.8	—37.3	—33.73	N.W. Vble. W. Calm. N.	0—1
3	—29	—35	—31.53	S.W. Calm. Vble.	0—1
4	—19	—26.5	—22.67	Calm. Vble. Calm.	0—1
5	—14	—20	—16.71	N.W. by S.	4—6
6	—14.7	—22.5	—17.5	N.	3—6
7	—22.5	—27	—25.16	Calm. N. by W. Calm.	0—1
8	—22.3	—30.5	—26.25	N. by W. N.N.W.	1—4
9	—20	—25.5	—21.65	N.W. N.W. by W.	1—6
10	—20	-—27	—23.35	N. Vble. N. by W.	0—2
11	— 8.7	—18.3	—11.64	W.N.W. N. by W.	1—6
12	—18	—23.5	—20.25	N. by W.	8—6
13	—35.3	—38	—36.83	N.N.W. N. by W.	7—2
14	—26	—36.5	—31	N.W.	6—3
15	—37.5	—42	—39.83	N.	4—7
16	—36.5	—42	—39.14	N. by W.	7—5
17	—35.5	—40.5	—38.4	N. N. by W. N.W.	7—3
18	—27.5	—34.5	—30.57	N. N. by W. N.N.W.	1—7
19	—22	—32.5	—27.57	N. Vble. S.S.E.	4—1
20	—22.5	—27.5	—25.3	N. by W. N. N.N.W.	7—4
21	—19.5	—27	—22.83	N.N.W. N. S.E.	3—1
22	—13	—26.5	—18.85	N.E. N.N.W.	1—5
23	—23.5	—31.5	—26.57	N.N.W. N.	3—1
24	—23	—34.5	—27.43	W. W. by N. N. N.W.	1—4
25	— 9.5	—27.5	—20.2	W. Calm. Vble.	1—0
26	— 9.3	—22	—13.5	S.E. E. E. by N. N.	1—2
27	—24	—27.5	—25.54	N.W. by N. N.N.W.	4—6
28	—34.5	— 40	—39.2	N.N.W. N.W. by W.	6—3
			746.85		
			—26.68		

Meteorological Journal for February, 1847.

Barometer and Thermometer attached.		Remarks on the Weather, &c.
Barom.	*Thermo.*	
29.901	+ 7.6	b. m. b. q. drifting.
30.023	+ 5.3	b. b.
30.593	+ 2.6	b. c. o. cirrus and cirro-stratus.
30.219	+ 5	b. c.
30.339	+ 5.6	b. c. q. much refraction; drifting.
30.18	+11.	b. c. m. b. c. drifting.
30.224	+12.	b. c. cirrus; cloudy near horizon.
30.418	+10.3	b. m. spiculæ. much refraction.
30.432	+12.	o. m. b. c. m. drifting; solar halo with parhelia; a faint arch of aurora.
30.065	+ 8.3	b. c. cirrus; some faint beams of aurora south and south-south-west (say south-west).
29.865	+12.6	b. c. m. o. s. b. c. s. drifting.
29.71	+12.	b. m. much drift.
29.644	+10.5	b. m. b. drifting.
29.65	+10.	b. m. b.
29.816	+12.6	b. b. m. b. drifting.
29.899	+13.3	b. m. b. much drift.
29.84	+ 7.6	b. m. b. drifting.
29.869	+ 7.3	b. c. o. b. c. m. much drift.
29.9	+ 6.7	b. c. s. o. m. Solar halo with prismatic colours and parhelia.
29.9	+ 8	b. m. b. drifting.
30.329	+ 7	b. c. b. c. m.
30.276	+ 9.6	b. m. b. c. s. o. s. b. c. s. drifting.
30.459	+ 9.3	b. m. b. c. cirrus; Venus visible for the first time, the horizon having been too hazy to see her sooner.
30.326	+ 7	b.
30.008	+ 6	b. b. c. much refraction.
30.221	+ 8.3	b. m. c. b. c. s.
30.146	+12	b. m. c. b. c. s. b. c. m. drifting along the ground.
30.073	+11	b. m. drifting.

FORT HOPE, REPULSE BAY.—*Abstract of*

Day of the Month.	Temperature of the Atmosphere taken eight times in twenty-four hours.			Prevailing Winds.	
	Highest.	Lowest.	Mean.	Direction.	Force.
	deg.m.	deg.m.	deg.m.		
1	—30.5	— 45	—37.5	N.byW. Chble. N.W.byN.	0—2
2	—30.5	—40.5	—35.4	N.W. by N. N.N.W.	2—4
3	—30	—37	—33.7	N.W. by N. N.N.W.	4—7
4	—27	—38	—32	N. by W. N.W. by N.	4—7
5	—26	—33	—28.4	N. by W. N.W. by N.	8—6
6	—27	—33	—29.4	N. by W.	8—4
7	—27.5	—37	—33	N.N. ½ E.	7—5
8	—25	—31.5	—27.5	N. N. by W. N.N.W.	7—9
9	—20	—30.5	—25.3	N.N.W. N.W. by N.	4—2
10	—21	—33.5	—27.2	N.W. N.N.W.	1—4
11	—10.7	—27.5	—20	N.W. by N. N. by W.	1—3
12	—19.5	—30.5	—23.7	N.N.W. N. N. by W.	8—10
13	—15	—19.5	—16.5	N.N.W.	10—12
14	—13.5	—15	—14.5	N. by W.	11—7
15	—11	— 19	—14.2	N. N.N.W.	8—5
16	— 7.7	—19	—11.7	N.W. by N. N. by W.	3—6
17	—24	—30	—26.5	N. W.N.W. W.	1—6
18	—18.7	—37.5	—29.1	Calm. S.S.E. W.	0—6
19	—14	—29.5	—21.4	W. Vble.	2—1
20	—23.5	—32.5	—29.1	N.N.W. N. N. by W.	6—4
21	—23	—29.5	—25.9	W.N.W.	10—7
22	—16	—27	—21.6	N W. by N. W.	6—1
23	—16	—33	—22.6	N.W. Chble. N. by W.	1—6
24	—29	—33.5	—30.9	N. by W. N.N.W.	9—7
25	—27	—35	—30.4	N. by W. N.N.W.	7—9
26	—26.5	—35.5	—30.6	N. by W.	6—8
27	—24.5	—34	—28.1	N. by W. N.N.W.	6—8
28	—26	—35	—30.2	N. by W.	2—7
29	—22	—33	—26.37	N.N.W. N. W.N.W.	8—5
30	—15	—32	—20.54	N.W. N. by W.	2—6
31	— 6	—14	— 8.6	N.N.W. N.W. by N.	7—6
			811.91		
			—28.1		

Meteorological Journal for March, 1847.

Barometer and Thermometer attached.		Remarks on the Weather, &c.
Barom.	*Thermo.*	
30.152	+ 4.3	b. b.
30.296	+ 4	b.
30.268	+ 4.6	b. m. drifting. The wind between noon and 2 P.M. went round for a few minutes, and then went back to its old direction.
30.399	+ 6.3	b. m. drifting.
30.492	+ 7	b. m. b. c. m. much drift.
30.63	+11.3	b. c. m. drifting.
30.514	+10.5	b. m. drifting.
30.232	+ 7.6	b. c. m. much drift.
30.194	+ 8	b. b. c.
30.179	+ 4	b. b. c. cirrus.
30.305	+ 4.7	b.
30.449	+ 9.7	b. m. much drift.
30.089	+ 7	b. q. thick drift.
30.07	+ 5	b. m. q. b. c. m. much drift.
30.886	+13	b. c. m. q. b. c. m. o. m. drifting.
29.578	+12	o. s. b. c. s. b. c. drifting.
29.814	+ 6.6	b. c. b. q. drifting.
29.99	+ 4.6	b. c. m. Solar halo with prismatic colours; drifting.
30.001	+ 5.6	b. m. b. c. cirrus.
29.569	+ 8	b. m. b. c. m.
29.372	+ 3	o. s. o. m. b. m. drifting.
29.673	+ 5	b. c. m. q. cirrus.
29.823	+ 6.7	b. c. m. o. s. Spiculæ; halo with prismatic colours; drifting.
29.854	+ 3.7	b. m. b. c. m. much drift; door drifted up.
29.899	+ .7	b. m. c. m. much drift; door drifted up.
30.196	+ 1.3	b. c. m. drifting.
30.046	— .3	b. m. b. c. m. drifting.
30.161	+ 1	b. m. c. drifting.
30.142	+ 2	b. m. drifting.
30.182	+ 3.5	b. c. m. o. m. drifting.
30.867	+10.6	b. c. m. b. c. s. o. s. drifting.

FORT HOPE, REPULSE BAY.—*Abstract of*

Day of the Month.	Temperature of the Atmosphere taken eight times. in twenty-four hours.			Prevailing Winds.	
	Highest.	Lowest.	Mean.	Direction.	Force.
	deg.m.	deg.m.	deg.m.		
1	— 6.5	—18.3	—11.57	N.W. by W. W. by N.	3—6
2	— 0.5	—21	— 9.03	W. N.N.W. N.W.	2—4
3	+ 8	—23.5	— 6.7	Vble. Calm.	1—0
4	0	—13	— 4.5	N.W. by N. N.	2—1
5		—10		N. by W.	5
6	+11	—20	— 5.3	S.	4
7	+18	— 9	+ 3.67		
8	+20	— 2	+ 8.3		
9	+ 2	—12	— 5	N.N.W.	
10	+19	—15	+ 3.66	E.	
11	+10	—15	— 1.6	E.	
12	+16	—17	— 2	S.	
13	+21	—11	+ 5.3	N.N.W.	
14	+15	ᵧ 0	+ 6.6	W.	
15	— 7	—17	—11.3	N.N.W.	9
16	—10	—19	—15.3	N.	9
17	— 8	—22	—16.3	N.	
18	— 2	—20	—12	N.W.	
19	— 5	—25	—13.7	N.N.W.	....
20	— 5	—20	—12.67	N.	....
21	0	—22	—10.3	N.N.W.	
22	— 8	—22	—13.3	N. by W.	....
23	+17	—12	+ 1.67	Vble.	2
24	— 6	—10	— 4.3	N.W.	....
25	+ 7	— 2	+ 1	N.	
26	+ 5	—10	— 1.6	N.N.W.	....
27	+ 8	— 5	+ 2	N.N.W.	....
28	+10	— 3	+ 4	N.N.W.	....
29	+11	— 1	+ 4	N.N.W.	....
30	+20	— 1	+ 9.6	N.	....
			122.57		
			— 3.95		

Meteorological Journal for April, 1847.

Barometer and Thermometer attached.		Remarks on the Weather, &c.
Barom.	Thermo.	
29.83	+10	b. c. m. drifting.
29.709		b. b. c.
29.708	+ 4	b. b. c. Barometer not registered after this. Thermometer with colourless rose to 5° only, although freely exposed to the sun's rays. At 8 P.M. a faint aurora of an orange colour; centre south; alt. 5°.
....	....	o. m. b. c. s. os.
....	....	o. s.
....	....	much drift all day.
....	....	much drift.
....	....	much drift and snow.
....	....	thick drift and snow. Some partridges seen.
....	....	drifting.
....	....	drifting thick.
....	....	snow and drift.
....	....	drifting.
....	....	drifting.
....	....	drifting.
....	....	drifting.

Fort Hope, Repulse Bay.—*Abstract of*

Day of the Month.	Temperature of the Atmosphere taken three times in twenty-four-hours.			Prevailing Winds.	
	Highest.	Lowest.	Mean.	Direction.	Force.
	deg.m.	deg.m.	deg.m.		
1	+20	+ 4	+11.6	W.	....
2	+20	+ 5	+12	N.	....
3	+17	+ 4	+ 9.3	N. by W.	....
4	+10	+ 0	+ 3.3	N.N.W.	....
5	+10	− 4	+ 3.67	N.N.W.	....
6	+23	0	+ 9.3	Vble. Calm.	1—2
7	+24	− 1.5	+10.5	S.E. E.	2
8	+23	+ 6	+14.8	Vble. E. S.S.E.	1—3
9	+26	+16	+18.5	S.E. E.	2—6
10	+19.5	+12	+15.67	E. by S. E.N.E.	6—10
11	+32.3	+18.5	+24.6	S. by E. S.W. W.N.W.	1—6
12	+25.5	+10	+15.93	N.W.	2—6
13	+25	+ 4.5	+11.5	W.	7—6
14	+33	+18	+23.3	S.W.	
15	+17	+10	+12.67	N.	....
16	+15	+ 9	+11.3	N.W.	....
17	+20	+15	+17	W.N.W.	
18	+30	+15	+21.67	N.W.	
19	+40	+18	+27.6	S.	
20	+37	+21	+27.3	N.	
21	+28	+18	+21.3	N.	11
22	+22	+16	+18.3	N.	10
23	+25	+16	+21	N.	10
24	+33	+26	+28.66	N.E.	
25	+43	+23	+30.67	N.E. by N.	
26	+34	+24	+27.67	N.N.E.	
27	+28	+21	+24.66	N.	....
28	+25	+16	+20	N.W.	
29	+45	+18	+28	S.	
30	+43	+24	+30.67	S.E.	....
31	+23	+18	+21	N.	....
			553.44		
			+17.88		

Meteorological Journal for May, 1847.

Barometer and Thermometer attached.		Remarks on the Weather, &c.
Barom.	*Thermo.*	
....	....	Newman's improved Cistern Barometer used.
....	....	{ Correction for capacities — $\frac{1}{54}$ Neutral point —30.302. Capillary action +.042. Temperature +60°.
....	....	A snow bird seen.
....	....	drifting.
....	....	drifting.
....	....	b. c.
....	....	o. s. b. c. s.
....	....	o. s. An inch of snow fallen.
....	....	o. s. o. o.
....	....	o. s and drifting thick.
....	....	o. s. pools of water. Beautiful evening.
....	....	b. c. drifting.
....	....	b. c. o. m.
....	....	fine weather.
....	....	thick weather.
....	....	Much snow drift.
....	....	Much snow and snow drift.
....	....	Much snow drift.
....	....	Snow and drift until evening.
....	....	Cloudy with snow.
....	....	Strong gale with drift.

FORT HOPE, REPULSE BAY.—*Abstract of*

Day of the Month.	Temperature of the Atmosphere taken three times in twenty-four hours.			Prevailing Winds.	
	Highest.	Lowest.	Mean.	Direction.	Force.
	deg.m.	deg.m.	deg.m.		
1	+25	+12	+19.3	S.	
2	+35	+17	+25.3	N.	....
3	+26	+14	+20	N.	
4	+32	+14	+21.7	N.W.	
5	+29	+18	+22	N.W.	
6	+43	+21	+28.3	Vble.	
7	+28	+18	+22	N.	
8	+30	+16	+22.7	N.	
9	+38	+24	+30.6	N.N.W. and Vble.	3—5
10	+39	+26	+31.3	N. and N.N.E.	1—3
11	+34	+28.5	+30.8	Vble. N.	1—6
12	+35	+26.5	+30.7	N. by W.	6—8
13	+37	+27	+32.3	N.	5—7
14	+40	+29.5	+34	N. by E.	2—4
15	+43.5	+26	+35.5	E. Vble. S.W.	2—3
16	+39.5	+36	+37.3	N. N.W.	4—2
17	+37	+30.5	+34	E. by S. S.E.	3—1
18	+38.5	+32.5	+34.67	E. N.E.	2—5
19	+34.5	+31	+32.5	N.N. by W.	7—9
20	+37	+33.5	+34.8	W.N.W.	10—11
21	+45.5	+33	+37.66	W. by N. S.E.	9—6—5
22	+40.5	+32	+35.1	N. N.N.W. N.W.	8—7
23	+42	+32.5	+36.2	W·N.W.	6—4—2
24	+46.5	+33	+38.73	Calm. Vble. S.E.	0—2
25	+36.7	+32.5	+34.23	E. by S.	3—4
26	+37	+31.3	+33.66	E.S E. E. by N. N.E.	6—9
27	+34.3	+31	+32.6	N.W. W·N.W.	10—11
28	+34	+31.5	+32.83	W. W. by N. W.N.W.	9—8
29	+37.3	+33.7	+35	N.W. N.W. by W.	10—8—0
30	+41	+32.3	+35.6	W.N.W. N.W. N.	7—8
			942.51		
			+31.38		

Meteorological Journal for June, 1847.

Barometer and Thermometer attached.		Remarks on the Weather, &c.
Barom.	*Thermo.*	
....	....	A strong gale.
....	....	b. c. m. Arrived at the house from our journey at 8h. 20m. A.M. by watch, or 7h. 20m. true time.
....	....	b. c.
....	....	o. s.
....	....	o. s.
....	....	o. p. s.
....	....	o. b. c.
....	....	b. c. p. sleet.
....	....	b. c.
....	....	b. c. p. o. r. First rain this spring.
....	....	o. r. o. f. o. r.
....	....	s. o. r. o.
29.480	+37	p. r. b. c. b. c. p. r. b. c.
29.817	+49	b. c. q. o. r.
30.289	+40	o. b. c. p. s. Showers of snow and sleet during the night.
30.14	+40.3	o. b. c. Saw sun at midnight, lower limb touching the high ground.
30.147	+46.5	b. c.
30.04	+40	o. o. f. A few flakes of snow falling.
29.68	+38.7	o. s. o. w. s. Half inch of snow during the night. Wet snow.
29.273	+37	o. s. o. p. s. q. From 6 to 8 inches of snow during the night.
29.39	+35.6	b. c. q. o. s. q.
29.488	+40	o. p. s. q. b. c. q. b. c. p. s.
29.61	+38	o. s. b. c. p. s. q. b. c. p. r. q. Wet snow.

FORT HOPE, REPULSE BAY.—*Abstract of*

Day of the Month.	Temperature of the Atmosphere taken three times in twenty-four hours.			Prevailing Winds.	
	Highest.	Lowest.	Mean.	Direction.	Force.
	deg.m.	deg.m.	deg.m.		
1	+39	+29.3	+33.6	N.N.W. N. by W. N.	4—6
2	+38	+31.3	+34.6	N. N.W. by N. N.W.	7—4
3	+46.5	+32	+38.17	W. Calm.	7—6—0
4	+35.5	+33	+34.1	N.E.	6—5—4
5	+45.5	+35	+39.8	W.	5—3—6
6	+46	+34	+39.17	W.N.W. N. by W. Chble.	7—0
7	+49	+38	+43	E. by S. S.E. Calm.	2—4—0
8	+51	+35	+42	E. E.S.E. E.	3—5—1
9	+48.7	+32.3	+38.7	N. Vble. E.	5—2
10	+41	+35	+37.17	E.S.E.	5—6
11	+36	+33	+34.5	E. by N. Calm.	4—3—0
12	+39.3	+35	+36.7	N. N. by E.	3—5—6
13	+38	+33.5	+35.6	N. by W. N.	8—9
14	+38	+33.7	+35.23	N.	9
15	+42.5	+34	+37.2	N. by W.	9—10
16	+39	+35.3	+37.7	N. Calm.	10—7—0
17	+46	+36	+42.5	N.N.W. W. by N.	8—5—3
18	+43	+35	+39.5	Vble. Calm.	3—4—0
19	+47.3	+36	+41.6	N.W.	5—6—3
20	+55.5	+41	+46.9	N.N.W. N.W. Calm.	3—5—0
21	+57	+44	+49.17	N. Vble. N.N.W.	4—1—3
22	+47	+40	+42.5	Calm. N.N.W.	0—6—5
23	+49.3	+38.5	+43.26	N.N.W. N. N. by W.	8—7—8
24	+48	+36.5	+41.9	N. N.W. by N.	9—7—3
25	+52	+36	+43.16	N.W. Calm.	6—4—0
26	+43	+38	+40.2	S.S.E. E.S.E. E.	2—6
27	+51.5	+40	+44.17	N.E. Calm.	5—3—0
28	+60	+45	+51.8	W. W.N.W. W. by S.	2—3—2
29	+53.5	+47	.+50.2	N.	4—3—1
30	+55	+38.3	+46.6	W. by N. N.	4—8—10
31	+48	+37.5	+42.5	N. by W.	3—8—5
			1285.4		
			+41.46		

Meteorological Journal for July, 1847.

Barometer and Thermometer attached.		Remarks on the Weather, &c.
Barom.	Thermo.	
29.786	+39.83	b. c. p. s. a little frost during the night.
29.838	+35.5	b. c.
29.986	+46	b. c. a beautiful night.
29.864	+40.3	o. p. o. f. p. r. o. sleet.
30.015	+43	b. c.
30.124	+42	b. c. b. c. q. Ther. at midnight +35°; coat of ice on pools where there is snow.
30.216	+49.5	b. c.
30.185	+46	b. c.
30.216	+40.3	o. b. c. o.
30.024	+42	o. b. c. o.
29.828	+42	p. r. f. o. f. w. o. Heavy rain during the night; wet fog and showers of rain.
29.802	+40	o. f. p. r. o. w. f.
29.938	+39	o. f. p. r. o. f. o. p. r. q.
29.968	+41.3	r. o. b. c. o.
29.905	+41.7	o. b. c. o. r. A great quantity of water coming down N. Pole River this morning; sleet.
29.865	+44.2	p. w. s. q. o. s. b. c. Snow showers all night; ther. at 6 P.M. +45°.
29.902	+47.2	o. b. c. at 5 P.M. Ther. at +54°.
		b. c. b. c. o.
29.716	+48	b c. q.
29.714	+56	b c.
29.776	+54.5	b. c.
29.794	+46.5	o. b. c. p. r. b. c.
29.791	+46	d. r. b. c. p. r. b. c.
29.858	+45.5	b. c.
29.967	+53	b. c.
29.815	+47.2	b. c. b. c. q.
29.917	+49	b. c.
30.038	+53.5	b. c.
30.113	+56.8	b. c.
30.017	+49	b. c. p. r. The barometer fell some hundredths lower than when registered at 6 A.M., but immediately began to rise as soon as the wind changed to the north.
30.102	+51.5	b. c.

FORT HOPE, REPULSE BAY.—*Abstract of*

Day of the Month.	Temperature of the Atmosphere taken three times in twenty-four hours.			Prevailing Winds.	
	Highest.	Lowest.	Mean.	Direction.	Force.
	deg.m.	deg.m.	deg.m.		
1	+52	+40	+44.8	N.	4—6—3
2	+56	+40	+47.7	N.N.W.	6—2—1
3	+49	+44.5	+46.2	N.W. N.N.W.	6—7—5
4	+41	+34.7	+36.9	N.N.W. N.	9—8
5	+54	+34	+62.5	N. N. by W.	7—6—3
6	+50	+46.5	+49.8	Vble. W.S.W.	3
7	+59.3	+43.5	+49.3	S.W. Calm.	4—5—0
8	+49.5	+42	+45.5	Vble. 'N.W.	1—2—6
9	+44.5	+37	+39.83	N. N.W.	8—6—4
10	+37.5	+35		N.	9—10—8

Meteorological Journal for August, 1847.

Barometer and Thermometer attached.		Remarks on the Weather, &c.
Barom.	*Thermo.*	
30.054	+56	b. c.
30.057	+56.5	b. c.
30.051	+48.5	b. c. q. p. r.; at 5 P.M. a heavy squall and showers of rain.
29.93	+41.5	b. c. q. p. s.
30.169	+46.5	b. c. ; frost last night.
30.124	+54	b. c. Ther. at 5 P.M. +62°—; all the large and deep lakes still covered with ice.
30.035	+61	b. c. q.
29.806	+54	o. p. r.
29.882	+47	b. c. q.
29.732	+43	o. r. s. s. b. c.

Figures and Letters used for denoting the state of the Weather and the force of the Wind, as recommended by Captain (now Admiral) Beaufort.

0—Calm.
1—Light air.
2—Light breeze.
3—Gentle breeze.
4—Moderate breeze.
5—Fresh breeze.
6—Strong breeze.
7—Moderate gale.
8—Fresh gale.
9—Strong gale.
10—Whole gale.
11—Storm.
12—Hurricane.

b.—Blue sky.
c.—Cloudy.
d.—Drizzling rain.
f.—Foggy.
g.—Gloomy dark weather.
h.—Hail
l.—Lightning.
m.—Misty hazy atmosphere.
o.—Overcast.
p.—Passing temporary showers.
q.—Squally.
r.—Rain—continued rain.
s —Snow.
t.—Thunder.
u.—Ugly, threatening appearance of the weather.
v.—Visibility of distant objects whether the sky be cloudy or not.
w.—Wet dew.
. —Under any letter indicates an extraordinary degree.

MARCHANT SINGER & CO., Printers, Ingram-Court, Fenchurch-Street.